SHAKESPEARE'S
MEASURE FOR MEASURE

SHAKESPEARE'S
Measure for Measure

By

MARY LASCELLES

Distributed in U.S.A. by

John de Graff, Inc.
31 East 10th Street
New York 3, N. Y.

UNIVERSITY OF LONDON
THE ATHLONE PRESS
1953

Published by
THE ATHLONE PRESS
at the Senate House, London, W.C.1

Distributed by Constable & Co. Ltd.
12 Orange Street, London, W.C.2

PR
2824
.L3

Printed in Great Britain by
WESTERN PRINTING SERVICES LTD.
Bristol

To
KATHLEEN TILLOTSON

PREFACE

INDEBTEDNESS for help with a book that has been long in writing lends itself poorly to formal expression. I hope that I have profited by Professor F. P. Wilson's advice one half as much as I have valued it. The many friends whose patience I must have taxed by apparently inconsequent questions and propositions would (I surmise) rather go unthanked than be named here.

Debts to published work I have of course acknowledged in the usual way, by reference in text or footnotes; but, as I look back over these references, they seem not to tell the story truly. The most stimulating antagonist for an admirer of *Measure for Measure* is not even named; but there is no arguing with Bridges: you bow to the magnificence of his language and his aristocratic temper, and then—if you cannot agree—seek another road. Johnson's name, on the other hand, may be thought to occur too often; but that is because I believe that modern criticism owes more to his comments on the play than the critics themselves recognize: surprise and petulance are the emotions most apparent when recognition is inescapable. Besides, veneration for his critical sagacity compels me to attend to what he says, even when I believe him to be in error.

Many objections will be found levelled against the edition of the play in the New Cambridge Shakespeare. Their aim must not be misunderstood. They imply no want of recognition of the value of that body of work of which it is a part—perhaps, not an entirely representative part. They are there because this is the edition most relevant to my argument: the most considerable, the most influential and, in its handling of the text, the most radical, of recent years. And my aim is to show that, however little I may have been able to contribute to the emendation of this text, it is not past mending, and is well worth the labour. The suggestions as to particular passages which I offer in an Appendix are designed to illustrate the narrow margin by which some obscure lines are separated from intelligibility, and the insignificance of some discrepancies.

I have to acknowledge a grant from the Leverhulme Research Fellowships in 1945, and a term's leave of absence from Somerville College.

M.M.L.

CONTENTS

Preface — page vii

Introduction — 1

Chapter I. Illustrations — 6

Chapter II. The Position Occupied by 'Measure for Measure' — 29

Chapter III. The Play Considered
- I. THE CASE — 43
- II. THE DISPUTANTS — 64
- III. THE ARBITER — 89
- IV. THE VERDICT — 122

Chapter IV. Conclusion — 139

Appendix — 165

Index — 169

A NOTE ON REFERENCES

ALL quotations from *Measure for Measure* show the Folio text; all references are given to the Globe text. For all other Shakespearian quotations and references the Globe text has been used.

Where I refer to any of Johnson's notes, I give Act-scene reference from his *Shakespeare* (1765), followed by Act-scene-line reference to the Globe.

For Whetstone's *Promos and Cassandra*, I have used the edition of 1578. For two other plays, frequently mentioned but seldom quoted—Middleton's *Phoenix* and Davenant's *The Law against Lovers*—I have referred the reader to standard modern editions: Bullen's of Middleton's works, Maidment and Logan for Davenant's. In default of such an edition for a third play in like case—Gildon's *Measure for Measure, or Beauty the Best Advocate*—I have used the quarto of 1700.

INTRODUCTION

No one, I suppose, has ever read or seen *Measure for Measure* without experiencing some bewilderment. Even on first acquaintance, the variety of impressions which the play generates is disquieting; and graver vexation awaits the resolute inquirer. Intimations of the play's significance seem to be proffered, and presently denied; a character assumes substance, even such density as is to be found nowhere else but in Shakespearian tragedy—only to surrender it and lapse into two dimensions. 'In a great work,' Johnson says, 'there is a vicissitude of luminous and opaque parts, as there is in the world a succession of day and night.' Though spoken of Milton, this has a plain bearing on Shakespeare and the varying tension by which drama accommodates itself to human capacity; but it is part only of a larger proposition: 'In every work one part must be for the sake of others.'[1] Are the parts of *Measure for Measure* recognizably co-operative? Do they not rather appear sometimes to defeat one another's purpose?

If the reader should turn for enlightenment to the critics, his perplexity would merely be increased. Not only is there diversity of opinion; there is sharp opposition, so sharp that he must sometimes make an effort to assure himself that they are speaking about the same play, for the difference is not merely of degree, nor does there seem to be any hope of reconciliation. What is he to think when two men of the stature (for example) of R. W. Chambers and Sir Edmund Chambers stand over against one another, one maintaining that the significance and temper of *Measure for Measure* are explicitly and unquestioningly Christian, the other that its atmosphere is one of thick darkness, illuminated only by the lightning that strikes all humanity alike and glances even towards divine providence?

[1] *Lives of the Poets*, ed. G. B. Hill (Oxford, 1905), i. 187.

What effrontery it then appears to offer an interpretation of this play—what folly, to add yet another to the already far too many books on Shakespeare! Why attempt to swell superfluity, and with so small prospect of success? To such questions this book must of course itself give the answer; if an answer could have been given more briefly, the book need not have been written. But mere civility to the reader asks at least some explanation of the devotion of a whole book to a single play—and all the more for this reason: any book involves partnership between writer and reader, and in the particular partnership I propose the reader's patience will be required. Not on account of difficulty: difficult as the play is, what I have to say is at bottom simple, and it can be said simply if it is said slowly. It is the reader's consent to slow progress that I require, together with a suspension of judgement for so long as the case is under consideration, and a resolute effort to lighten memory of certain associations, accompaniments to the reading of Shakespeare's plays so habitual that their presence goes unnoticed. There are for us now two big impediments to understanding, particularly of those plays which may be for convenience called romantic, because they are founded on extant romances—that is, on fictitious narrative. One of these impediments is so insidious that it is hard to recognize; the other, so obvious that it is hard to take it seriously.

Between us and Elizabethan drama stands a familiarity with the novel which, being early formed and lying deep, is seldom taken into conscious reckoning. Furthermore, it is romantic novels with which we first become acquainted, and the English[1] romantic novel is directly sprung from the English way of reading Shakespeare. Thus our reactions to his plays have been insensibly modified by those very changes which are a condition of life for their offspring.

The other difficulty is likely to appear ridiculous when first formulated: we are possessed of information at once too full and too partial. These plays, I believe, were more intelligible to those who first discovered their connections and origins than they are to us, because the discoverers not only found, but continued to read, the stuff of which Shakespeare had made use *in its proper context*,

---

[1] Some apology is due for including Scott; but who, within these islands, would be better pleased with the term British?

INTRODUCTION

the context familiar alike to dramatist and audience; they read it in those collections (original or translated) in which it was available to the Elizabethan reader.[1] And, by a minor irony of circumstance, their discoveries opened the way to such scholarly labours as have done scholarship a sort of disservice: to reprints of single tales from those collections, and even of passages from those tales, and extracts from those passages—all designed to smooth the reader's way to understanding. Perhaps it would be too much to say that, the more our convenience is consulted, the more helpless we become—but hardly too much to guess that, when what we immediately need has been made available, we may not look beyond or beside it. Will not the candid reader admit that he has had, at some instant or other, to shrug himself awake and dispel the illusion that Shakespeare found the stories for his plays in a row of compact volumes labelled 'Shakespearian sources'? And the unhappy consequence of our situation is wasteful division among Shakespearian scholars. The eager young researcher seeks more and more widely—and, to the unsympathetic eye, distractedly—for analogues, versions of his originals with which Shakespeare may or may not have been acquainted; while the established critic develops a princely indifference to all such inquiries, all attempts to dig in the soil whence the plays grew—careless of former cultivation, or disappointed with the crop. I therefore beg the reader to lay aside both his remembrance of acknowledged sources in convenient reprints, and impatience with this digging—at least until the sod has been turned afresh and the tissue of roots laid bare.

If, in what I have to say, I should seem to attend too little to those who have tilled this soil before me, it will not be for want of attention to what they have reported. I have listened, followed their directions, and even found small objects hitherto unnoticed —only to doubt their significance, and wish that the nature of this sort of evidence might be considered afresh. Names of characters, for example, are surely a very dubious way of tracing the footsteps of a writer of fiction 'in other men's snow'.[2] And there is not

[1] Malone and Douce, for example, between them owned a big proportion of those books I shall have occasion to mention; their references often reflect the easy familiarity of ownership.

[2] Arguments based on the names of characters in *Measure for Measure* have been discounted by the observation that Shakespeare had already used them elsewhere.

always more satisfaction to be got from enumeration of similar incidents: it means little unless we can find a way of differentiating between such details as any story-teller is likely to introduce, amplifications governed by necessity or convention, and such as will hardly present themselves to his imagination unless at another man's prompting.

Let me illustrate briefly one possibility of error. Amongst the stories cited by Gaston Paris as analogues to *Cymbeline*,[1] there is one group of which the characteristic pattern may be outlined thus: a woman deals with a dishonourable proposal (the result of her husband's wager on her fidelity) by feigning compliance and sending another woman in her place. Presently, on an occasion contrived by her husband to bring her to open shame for the infidelity of which he now believes her guilty, she turns the tables on him and on her adversary, proving that it was not she who kept the assignation; and the other woman, who has 'steaded up her appointment', is given the choice between exacting the forfeit due from the man who has wronged her (his life), and marrying him. Set the initial wager aside, and this could be added to the analogues of *Measure for Measure*, but what would it signify? Only the inexhaustible scope and eventual futility of such inquiry, which, if pushed beyond the bounds of common sense, must concern itself with crude elements of narrative possessing, in common with other low forms of life, the power of apparently effortless increase. It would be possible, by the exercise of tireless ingenuity, either to make it appear that one or another of Shakespeare's romantic plays contains within itself almost every known type of romantic incident; or, to show that the variants of a single type of romantic tale, boldly deployed, will furnish incidents for all of his romantic plays. I believe it is better to launch out beyond reach of soundings than to ferry for ever across and across these land-locked waters of research.

For significant resemblances between Shakespeare's plays and such stories as he may well have known, we must turn to characteristics less patient of arithmetic. It is not by dress, or even feature,

---

[1] 'Le Cycle de la Gageur' (*Romania*, xxxii, Paris, 1903). See, further, the ballad version of this story: Child, *English and Scottish Ballads* (Boston and New York, 1882), v. 268.

that we recognize an acquaintance, but by build, carriage and gait. And it is for the equivalent of build, carriage and gait that we must look, when works of imagination are to be compared together. I will not say that certainty lies this way. The impressions on which this sort of recognition depends, however lively they may be to the apprehension, remain very hard to analyse; and, at the last, interchange of opinions on the matter will be baffled by a residue of such conviction as springs from nothing more communicable, nor less personal, than taste. But the difficulty is not wilfully sought; it is inherent in literary criticism.

This, then, is what I propose: to use a manner as near narrative as the matter will allow—to move *towards* the play through a succession of possible sources and analogues, 'illustrations', as they used to be called; to maintain an unhurried motion *alongside* it, and hope to recapture something of the impression it may have left on the minds of that first audience, which saw and heard without knowing what was to come: undistracted by our knowledge of the play's outcome or its sequel, of the way in which Shakespeare was to conclude it, or the way in which he was to write when it was concluded.

I

ILLUSTRATIONS

'I scarcely remember ever to have looked into a book of the age of Queen Elizabeth, in which I did not find somewhat that tended to throw a light on these plays.'

(Malone, *Preface* to his edition of Shakespeare)

THE story of a woman compelled to treat for the life of a condemned man seems to be widespread, and various in form. The earliest of those forms bearing any resemblance to the plot of *Measure for Measure* which has come to notice is the anecdote of Acyndinus governor of Antioch, as it is related in St. Augustine's treatise *De Sermone Domini in Monte Secundum Matthaeum*.[1] Here is the gist of it: a man of Antioch being unable to pay the amount of tax due from him is threatened with death by Acyndinus. In this strait he allows his wife to sell herself to a former suitor for the sum required. This man defrauds his victim, delivering to her in payment a bag which contains not gold but dirt. She, in the bitterness of discovering how she has been used, tells all. Acyndinus is shocked into recognizing his own share of responsibility for what has happened, and, in acknowledgement of excessive severity, himself pays the tax; he moreover condemns the false suitor to make over to the woman the plot of ground from which her bag was filled.

Although this illustration of a problem in conduct was very likely known to Shakespeare's generation (Donne refers to it in *Biathanatos*,[2] and it would agree with contemporary taste for

[1] Liber Primus caput xvi. (Migne, *Patrologiae Latinae*, Paris, 1861, xxxiv. 1254.) That Douce knew of this, the manuscript note in the Bodleian copy of his *Illustrations of Shakespeare* (1807) witnesses, though the spelling of the name suggests that he may not have traced the story further back than Bayle.

[2] *Biathanatos* (1648), p. 127. I owe this reference to Miss Helen Gardner. For an examination of this fashion in paradox and problem, see Willard Farnham, *Shakespeare's Tragic Frontier* (University of California Press, 1950), in which it is conjectured that *Biathanatos* may have been written 'at some time between 1606 and 1609'.

formal paradox), yet no connection appears between this version of the story and the plain, brutal and calamitous tale which became current in Europe about the middle of the sixteenth century. A man lies in prison, at another's mercy—that other, sometimes his superior officer, more often a judge or magistrate, always a representative of constituted authority. The prisoner's wife intercedes with the judge, who, coveting her, proposes to her a monstrous way of ransoming her husband: if she will lie with him one night, his prisoner shall be delivered to her. Unwillingly she complies, and keeps her appointment; but the judge has treacherously ordained that night for the execution, and in the morning her husband's body is delivered to her. With nothing now to lose, past fear and past shame, she appeals to some higher authority—the captain or governor under whom her oppressor serves—for redress, and obtains sentence against him. He is to marry her, in reparation for the violation of her person, and to lose his life, for the violation of his faith to her. It may be convenient in referring back to this story-pattern to call it the *story of the monstrous ransom*.

Already at the beginning of the nineteenth century, Douce could instance a number of versions of this tale. Early in this century, Louis Albrecht[1] laboured exhaustively in the same field, claiming importance for yet another version. Presently, Mr. F. E. Budd[2] increased the number with a major claimant of his own discovery, and some minor analogies, giving besides a fuller account of the diversity among these versions. Their number is already formidable, and may yet increase; but distinction is possible: the degree of relevance varies. Popular or traditional versions can do little more than repeat the pattern; though they may amplify, they will hardly develop; and though the circumstances may alter (the prisoner being now a malefactor, now a victim, and the judge more, or less, culpable accordingly) the theme remains constant: a representation of wrong-doing and retribution, of power exerted to the utmost against weakness, and weakness at the last gathering

[1] *Neue Untersuchungen zu Shakespeares 'Mass für Mass'* (Berlin, 1914).
[2] In two articles: 'Rouillet's *Philanira* and Whetstone's *Promos and Cassandra*' (*Review of English Studies*, January 1930); and 'Material for a Study of the Sources of Shakespeare's *Measure for Measure*' (*Revue de Littérature Comparée*, October 1931). See also books and articles enumerated in '*Epitia*' and '*Measure for Measure*', by R. H. Ball (University of Colorado Studies, Series B, vol. 2, 1945).

itself up to appeal beyond power to authority. Literary versions, on the other hand, will bear the stamp of the individual imagination: according to each writer's vision the situation will be developed; and according to the measure of his power the burden which the tale carried for him will be communicated to us. It is these literary versions which should detain us.

If we consider the significant versions of this story in order of publication (so far as this can be ascertained), the first will be the *Philanira* of Claudius Roilletus, Mr. Budd's notable discovery.[1] Roilletus,[2] Principal of the Collège de Bourgogne, flourished in Paris in the mid-sixteenth century. He published in 1556 a volume of miscellaneous verse, *Varia Poemata*,[3] containing, together with some formal dialogues, epigrams and epithalamies, four plays. Three of these are on religious subjects; all may be described as neo-classical in form, though they do not observe strictly every convention of this kind. *Philanira*—perhaps, because its theme is neither scriptural nor legendary—is guarded by a brief prose preface and expounded in an Argument. A French version of it appeared in 1563, and again in 1577; this is attributed to Roilletus himself,[4] though he seems not to have acknowledged it. Mr. Budd's case for the significance of *Philanira* may be summed up in these terms: it is a romantic play, and, as such, to be regarded as forerunner and model for Elizabethan dramatists. This position is open to challenge. An irregularly formed classical play does not grow romantic—any more than an oddly shaped apple will grow into a pear. A dramatist does not write a romantic play by stretching or breaking a few of the conventions observed by ancient dramatists, or attributed to them by renaissance admirers. What Roilletus, in his preface, pleads with modesty and spirit is the right to deviate from the precepts of Horace, the practice of Seneca, as he thinks fit, and occasion requires. What he is doing is what all but the strictest neo-classicists were doing, each in his own way; but, as a scholar, he knows what he is about, and says so.

Philanira may be likened to a group of baroque statuary—figures

[1] See, in particular, his earlier article (*Review of English Studies*, January 1930), to which I am indebted for much information.
[2] Claude Roillet, or Rouillet.   [3] Paris.
[4] See *Les Bibliothèques Françoises de la Croix du Maine et de du Verdier Sieur de Vamprisius*, ed. Roley de Juvigny, 1772.

frozen in attitudes of extravagant animation. The rhetoric is highly wrought and declamatory; the emotional tone high-pitched; but nothing moves. The story follows the course I have described, with this sole addition; when sentence has been given on the unjust judge, his victim (Philanira) pleads vehemently for his life, and, failing, proclaims herself inconsolable and threatens suicide. The amplifications are all such as contemporary dramatic convention might suggest: a confidant for the judge, another for the ruler; two sympathetic handmaidens and three wailing children for Philanira; a messenger, and a Chorus prompt to say what the occasion demands. Although there is a time-interval (the fatal night), there is no indication of change of scene, and change of interest is deliberately avoided: the action is single and the tone unvaried.

The influence of *Philanira* cannot be measured until its successors have been surveyed. The first of them appears in that form so attractive to Elizabethan dramatists: the Italian *novella*. The fifth tale of the eighth day of Giraldi Cinthio's *Hecatommithi* tells, with bold variations, the tale of the monstrous ransom, and has generally been acknowledged a principal source, directly or indirectly, of *Measure for Measure*. The degree of indebtedness is indeed not in doubt, but the nature of the relationship asks fresh consideration.

Giovanni Battista Giraldi Cinthio,[1] a gentleman of Ferrara—administrator, scholar and man of letters—spent his more prosperous years under the patronage of the ducal house of Ferrara. This period drew to a close in 1560. His enemies took, as he thought, advantage of the death of his particular patron, Duke Hercole, and forestalled him in the favour of the new duke, Alfonso. Estrangement drove him to seek protection elsewhere. Established under the patronage of the house of Savoy, he published in 1565 the collection of tales on which he had been engaged since 1528: the *Hecatommithi*,[2] framed on the model of Boccaccio's *Decameron*. The setting is a voyage. In a distressful time, a party of fugitives from Rome makes a leisurely progress by water, occasion-

---

[1] See Louis Berthe de Besaucèle, *J-B. Giraldi, Etude sur l'Evolution des Théories Littéraires en Italie au XVIe Siècle* (Paris, 1920).

[2] *De gli Hecatommithi di M. Giovanbattista Giraldi Cinthio* (Mondovì, 1565). My references are to the second edition (Venice, 1566).

ally resting and holding a session, in which the disputants are supposed to illustrate with tales their estimates of human relationships. Sometimes these tales are closely connected with the theme of the day; sometimes that theme is so framed that a story of men and women can hardly miss illustrating it; sometimes the connection is tenuous. Weight is lent by three substantial *Dialoghi della vita Civile*. The prevailing tone is graver than that of the *Decameron*; there are, indeed, some tales of mere intrigue and adventure, but there is little humour, and the author seems happiest when he is engaged in just such romantic narrative as might furnish a plot for tragi-comedy—a form which he had ardently defended in his *Discorsi*.[1]

In his treatment of this tale, Giraldi's most notable innovation—that from which the rest seem to follow—is the change in the relationship of the victims: husband and wife to brother and sister, Vico[2] and Epitia. The tale is offered as an illustration of the theme which governs the eighth day's discourse, ingratitude.[3] Stirred by a foregoing account of benevolence ill rewarded, some of the company wonder that God allows such wrong-doers to live; but the more experienced conclude that he 'allows the wicked to continue among the good, in order that they may serve as a perpetual exercise of the others' virtue, and as it were a spur, to make them resort to him'. Furthermore, it is argued that magistrates, who are God's deputies in this world, ought to punish ingratitude as severely as they would crimes of which the law takes cognizance, homicide, adultery, theft. The tale of Epitia is told to show how such an act of ingratitude was punished by a ruler who thus performed his proper function—or would have been punished, but for the signal generosity of the victim.

From the outset, a slight but distinct emphasis is laid on the relation of this ruler (the Emperor Maximian) to the deputy whom he appoints, in his ordinary administrative course, to govern Innsbruck: Juriste. Maximian warns him of the responsibility that he

---

[1] Venice, 1554.
[2] The name appears as *Vieo* in several early editions: viz., 1565, 1566, 1584. Both *Vico* and *Vieo* occur in 1608. The correct form must be *Vico*; moreover, this is the form in Giraldi's play; see below.
[3] The word had then a wider sense: ill-doing of which the guilt is heightened by breach of obligation.

will incur by accepting office, but he lacks self-knowledge and is too much elated with the prospect of advancement to examine himself. Such individual traits as he is allowed are those of a customarily upright man with unsuspected springs of headstrong, unreflective greed. The culprit, Vico, likewise headstrong, is a mere boy. His offence is rape. His sister, Epitia, two years the elder, has shared with him the instruction of an old philosopher, and is clearly the more resolute spirit. In her approach to the judge, she relies on argument: her brother's offence has done no injury beyond what he can and will repair, and therefore, however the law may regard it, is in equity capable of pardon; it is, moreover, a magistrate's function thus to discriminate and give sentence accordingly. Juriste, however, intending ill, promises to ponder her argument and enjoins her presently to return. When she comes again for a decision, he confronts her with his monstrous proposal, hinting that he may perhaps make her his wife. Vico, when he learns of these terms, entreats his sister to ransom him, arguing that marriage will repair the wrong. Upon this stipulation she surrenders, but is betrayed; in the morning, her brother's body is delivered to her, with the severed head laid at the feet. Epitia, as one 'instructed in philosophy', conceals grief and anger and, after considering and rejecting a project of assassination, resolutely sets out alone in search of the absent Emperor, and finding him at Villaco tells him her whole tale. From this point to the close Maximian is present and active, but it is Epitia who determines the course of the action. When the Emperor has confronted Juriste with his victim, and when she has silenced his legalistic quibbling and convicted him of guilt, the forced marriage is decreed, and Epitia sent away that the second part of the sentence may be pronounced in her absence. But she, learning of it, reasons with herself as to the distinction between vengeance and justice, and, returning to the Emperor, re-opens the case. She is something of a doctrinaire, and something of a rhetorician (not infrequent accompaniments of heroic virtue among Giraldi's characters), but she praises mercy nobly and the Emperor is moved by her magnanimity, and allows her plea. We are told that Epitia and Juriste lived happily together.

The *Hecatommithi* has not as a whole been translated into English. A few of the tales appeared severally in Elizabethan collections,[1] but not (so far as is known) this tale of Epitia. It was to be read only in the complete *Hecatommithi* in Italian or in French. A French translation was made by Gabriel Chappuys, a man of letters and translator of wide repute, and appeared in two volumes, the tales of the first five days in 1583, the rest in 1584, under the title: *Cent Excellentes Nouvelles de M. Jean Baptiste Giraldy Cynthien*.[2] The three dialogues had meanwhile appeared separately in 1583, the French and Italian side by side: *Dialogues Philosophiques et tres-utiles Italiens-Francois, touchant la vie Civile*.[3] The tale of Epitia seems not to have been translated into English before the eighteenth century.[4]

This story Giraldi fashioned afresh as a play. The date cannot be ascertained, but it is generally considered late work, and may have been written not long before his death in 1573. It has been claimed as a likely source for Elizabethan versions.[5] True, it deviates from Giraldi's tale in that very direction which was presently to be taken by Whetstone and Shakespeare; but against this must be set its unpopular form and its inaccessibility: it was unlikely to please, and hard to come by. Giraldi's stage is crowded with figures, but not as the popular Elizabethan stage is crowded: there is no stir of life, no reflection of the many-coloured human scene; there is not even bustle. The throng is composed of intermediaries, by whom everything is transacted, without whom the principals can neither resolve nor act. Even Juriste has no motion of his own: he is a puppet in the hands of another character—one who exists only to prompt Juriste. Moreover, every event of consequence happens 'off', and the originator of the situation, Vico, never appears. Thus, the action is developed in narrative, to the accompaniment of voluble commonplaces by confidants and chorus.

[1] See M. A. Scott, *Elizabethan Translations from the Italian* (Boston and New York, 1916).
[2] Paris.
[3] Ever since George Steevens referred to it disparagingly in a note on *Othello* (Johnson's *Shakespeare*, 1773, x. 357 n. 1), it has been called faulty and incomplete. I can discover no reason for these charges. The separate publication of the Dialogues may explain them.
[4] Charlotte Lennox, in her *Shakespear Illustrated* (1753), gives a free version.
[5] See L. Albrecht, *Neue Untersuchungen zu Shakespeares 'Mass für Mass'*, and R. H. Ball, '*Epitia*' and '*Measure for Measure*'.

When *Epitia* opens, the three principal characters have come to an agreement and are expecting to enjoy its fruits. Vico is reprieved, and Epitia and Juriste are on the eve of a marriage to which an air of respectability is lent by the approval and good offices of Juriste's sister Angela, and the sympathetic concern of all the other characters but one. This one is the formidable Mayor of Innsbruck, a stickler for legality; and it is under his pressure that the colourless Juriste breaks faith, and, amid a tumult of unavailing entreaties and a confusion of orders and counter-orders, ordains the execution. Epitia is dissuaded from taking the law into her own hands by the counsels of her aunt Irene and the opportune arrival of the Emperor in Innsbruck. Having heard her tale, he calls Angela as witness, and it is this that eventually gives Juriste an advocate; for it is Angela who, horrified at having incriminated him, pleads on his behalf. Epitia is inexorable. At this juncture, an officer of justice, who has been hinting at a pleasant surprise in store, reports that, on the occasion of Vico's supposed execution, he took the liberty of substituting another man's head, and can therefore produce Vico whole.

Ten years after Giraldi's death, his son, Celso Giraldi, brought out a volume of his plays. In his dedication of *Epitia* to the Duchess of Ferrara he stated that this play had never been made public, either on the stage or in print. This dedication is dated 1583. Thus, until 1583, it was practically inaccessible to anyone outside the Giraldis' immediate circle, and even after publication it was available only in this single collection, which chance alone could have brought into English hands.

The acknowledged and principal source of *Measure for Measure*, among English versions of this story, is Whetstone's play, *Promos and Cassandra*,[1] published in 1578.[2] Like other Shakespearian sources, it has been reprinted[3] oftener than it intrinsically deserves,

---

[1] Whetstone has changed all names: Juriste becomes Promos; Epitia, Cassandra; Vico, Andrugio, and the Emperor Maximian, King Corvinus. Innsbruck becomes Julio.

[2] In his dedicatory epistle, dated 29 July 1578, Whetstone says: 'Of late I perused divers of my unperfect workes', this among them, leaving the reader to surmise how recently it had been begun.

[3] See: J. Nichols, *Six Old Plays* (1779); W. C. Hazlitt, *Shakespeare's Library* (1875); J. S. Farmer, *Tudor Facsimile Texts* (privately printed, 1910).

and this may have done it some disservice: it is seldom mentioned without disparagement. As a play, it is amateurish; as an illumination of the Elizabethan scene, and of the character of a man who played a part sometimes pitiable, sometimes ludicrous, but not altogether discreditable, *Promos and Cassandra* is a document which we cannot afford to neglect, nor even to read impatiently. George Whetstone's life[1] was, even by the standards of a dangerous age, short and unlucky. It used to be supposed that he was born in 1544. If his latest biographer is right, the date should be corrected to 1551, cutting off seven of his few years. He was a member of a prosperous family but, with his numerous brothers and sisters, was left orphaned, and for his own part was usually in wretched circumstances. Among his writings are scattered many urgent and high-pitched warnings to prodigals. These, it is true, are common enough in Elizabethan pamphlets; but in one of his didactic pieces (*A Touchstone for the Time*, 1584) Whetstone refers to another of these (*The Rocke of Regard*, 1576) in such terms as to suggest that its closing passage is autobiographical; and he often hints at dire experience. An unhappy characteristic marks all these passages, and is indeed perceptible throughout his work: it is evident that he thought of himself in the first place as a member of a particular social class, and (it is a frequent concomitant) believed that the world was very hard on this class. Society seemed to him so framed as to offer the largest possible temptations and the least possible rewards to young gentlemen of good family and high spirits. At a deeper level in his writings lies the evidence that he had known error and misfortune, and had lived among faulty and unlucky people.

Whetstone travelled and saw service abroad. He took part in Sir Humphrey Gilbert's disastrous voyage to Newfoundland in 1578–9. By his own account (in *The Honorable Reputation of a Souldier*, 1585) he had visited 'the Duchy of Millaine, and kingdome of Naples', and was prevented only by a quarrel with a Spaniard from entering Rome.[2] Like so many of his generation, he

---

[1] The fullest and most recent account is T. C. Izard's *George Whetstone* (New York, 1942), to which I owe much information.

[2] The date of Whetstone's Italian journey is fixed by references in three of his works: *The Honorable Reputation of a Souldier* (A. ii. ᵛ.); *The English Myrror* (1586, p. 156); *The Censure of a Loyall Subject* (1587, F. 4. ʳ). He was there in 1580.

went out to fight in the Low Countries; but, if this was not until 1587,[1] he was dead in a duel within a month of his arrival.

Need and a restless mind had driven Whetstone to literature. He seems to write with equal hurry in verse and prose. His published stuff, voluminous for so short a career,[2] may be considered in four groups. One, which is of no interest here, consists of verse obituaries on notable persons lately dead. A second, more variously composed, can best be described as the outpourings of a loyal and anxious citizen—warnings and exhortations addressed to all his fellow-countrymen, but most pointedly to magistrates and other civil authorities. These, being illustrated by narrative passages, merge with a third group: tales, gathered from many sources familiar to the needy scribbler of that age, tales romantic and ribald, sententious and scandalizing, offered with general professions of didactic intention. The fourth sort is represented by *Promos and Cassandra*, Whetstone's sole play. This touches the preceding group at one point, for Whetstone handled the story in narrative form also: as one of the tales[3] in his *Heptameron of Civil Discourses* (1582).[4]

The Right Excellent and famous Historye, of Promos and Cassandra: Devided into two Commicall Discourses is a play in two parts, of five acts each. A main plot, which tells a version of the story of the monstrous ransom, is accompanied by a sub-plot which, seeming to be of the dramatist's own devising and intended to serve as commentary, reflects his reading of this story. Whetstone's *Heptameron* is merely an inexpert imitation of such fashionable collections as the *Decameron* and the *Hecatommithi*.[5] The author represents himself as a traveller, benighted on Christmas Eve, and calling at a stranger's door to ask his way to Ravenna. The master of the house, 'Segnior Phyloxenus', hospitably constrains him to keep Christmas within, and to join in a formal session of debate and

[1] Mr. Izard argues that it was his elder brother, Bernard, who fought at Zutphen: op. cit., p. 28.
[2] Not, however, quite so voluminous as it appears; more than one work was re-issued with a fresh title-page.
[3] For reprints of this tale, see J. P. Collier, *Shakespeare's Library* (1843 [1850]), and W. C. Hazlitt, *Shakespeare's Library* (1875).
[4] Re-issued as *Aurelia* (1593).
[5] The 'Civil Discourses' composing it are designed as dialogues with narrative illustrations, bearing on man's life in society.

story-telling. His sister, Aurelia, appointed queen of the ceremonies, sets the company to debate the claims of the married and single state, with narrative illustrations. Their taste in these is not fastidious. Nevertheless, the general tenor of the work might fairly be represented by the opening of one of the song-interludes:

> Two Soveraigne Dames, Beautie and Honestie,
> Long mortal foes, accorded are of late.
> And now the one, dwels in my Mistresse eye,
> And in her hart the other keepes her state.[1]

At times, however, the debate descends (as such debates will) into mere wrangle between men and women; and it is a passage of this sort that gives rise to the tale of Promos and Cassandra.[2] The preceding illustration has been concerned with the intrigues of a friar, taken from the *Decameron* at its most anti-clerical. It is suggested that as much ill might be told of nuns. Whereupon 'Donna Isabella', who has been chosen arbiter on the women's side, undertakes to recount so black a tale against a man that nothing which can be said against women will counterbalance it. The story which follows agrees with the main plot of the play but retains no trace of the sub-plot; and the treatment is in every respect slighter.

Two questions are posed by Whetstone's versions of this story: what is the nature of their relationship to the several former versions, and what does he bring to it himself? Mr. Budd, who supposes him to owe something to Roilletus, has shown that *Philanira* was not unknown in Elizabethan England.[3] The evidence for its having been accessible to Whetstone is, however, slight: a reference to a performance at Cambridge when he was only thirteen,[4] the survival of a copy which was in the possession of an Englishman eight years after the publication of his own first treatment of the story—this may permit but does not encourage the belief in his acquaintance with it; and of this acquaintance I can find no mark in either version of *Promos and Cassandra*. Whetstone eagerly invokes precedent for what he means to do, in his dedicatory epistle, but it is precedent drawn from established comedy: Menander, Plautus and Terence are cited. If he had indeed known *Philanira*,

---
[1] G. iii ᵛ. (the second day).   [2] On the fourth day.
[3] 'Rouillet's *Philanira* and Whetstone's *Promos and Cassandra*' (*Review of English Studies*, January 1930, p. 47).   [4] Accepting Mr. Izard's date for his birth.

a treatment of the very theme he was attempting, in a convention which commanded the prestige of classical tragedy, surely he would have hesitated and endeavoured to explain himself?

The intention of *Promos and Cassandra* in both its forms is indubitably comic. The play, indeed, is doubly committed.[1] Its main plot conforms to a pattern which any mediaeval theorist would recognize for the pattern of comedy: it tells a story which moves from a sorrowful and fearful beginning to a happy and confident ending. Whetstone thus leans towards Giraldi's position. He accepts that relationship between the two in peril which seems to have originated with the *Hecatommithi*—brother and sister—and for *his* offence prefers rape to homicide, further softening the act by suggesting that it might be regarded as mutual consent between impatient lovers to anticipate marriage.[2] Thus Cassandra has from the first no doubt or scruple in pleading that the old law revived by Promos as the King's deputy in Julio is too severe; and when Andrugio urges that she may with a clear mind buy his life on the terms proposed by Promos, only stipulating for her own sake that marriage shall follow, she demurs but faintly, talks formally of reputation, and is easily reassured. Thenceforward, Whetstone's story follows a straighter course towards the happy ending than that of the *Hecatommithi*. A compassionate gaoler releases Andrugio, substituting for his head that of a man already dead. Meanwhile, until persuaded of her brother's death, Cassandra still looks for marriage with Promos, and when judgement has been delivered and the first part of Promos' sentence carried out she reproaches herself, and as his wife grieves bitterly that he should die. Moved by her grief, Andrugio intervenes and the King relents. Moreover, he does not hesitate to restore the penitent Promos to office and dignity.

Giraldi, then, rather than Roilletus governs the course of Whetstone's main plot—but Giraldi as author of *novella* or of play? Admittedly, where *Promos and Cassandra* departs from the course

[1] For a discussion of the double heritage of Elizabethan comedy, see Nevill Coghill, 'The Basis of Shakespearian Comedy', in *Essays and Studies* (English Association, 1950).

[2] He is not very clear or consistent in his references to it. In other versions of the story the condemned man lies under sentence for a variety of offences; but the commonest is some act of violence, involving homicide.

taken in the *Hecatommithi* it corresponds with *Epitia*; but this may prove a misleading correspondence. Before accepting *Epitia* as Whetstone's source we should have to suppose that he had visited Italy by 1578—it is strange, if so, that he should three times mention the 1580 visit and never this one—that he had become intimate with the younger Giraldi, and read a play which was lying in manuscript among his father's papers—read it through with close attention[1]—though of this whole experience no trace remains. This is a big supposition indeed; and to dispense with it Albrecht has to advance a bigger:[2] that Celso Giraldi was lying when he said in 1583 that the play had never been printed nor performed; there was a performance, or edition, of which no trace remains; or else, if Whetstone had not visited Italy by 1578, Giraldi's play in manuscript must have visited England. This is surely to suppose too much. It is besides unnecessary. Whetstone need not have been indebted to any particular source for the incident of the feigned execution; and his treatment of it differs a little from Giraldi's. If he required the assurance of literary precedent for using so common a device as the substituted victim, he had not to look further than the popular Greek romances.[3] Moreover, in *Promos and Cassandra*, Andrugio's transaction with his gaoler, his subsequent exile and the course by which he comes to intervene in Promos' trial are fully imagined and presented with such circumstance as Whetstone can command. In *Epitia*, on the other hand, we have a full but (as afterwards appears) false account of the execution from a messenger (presumably confederate with the officer responsible), and are left supposing it true until the final disclosure, also made in narration. Such motives as might prompt Whetstone to this alteration may have been shared by Shakespeare, and therefore can be considered presently.

Whetstone's contribution to the development of this story cannot be reckoned without some reference to the relationship between his two versions of it. Wanting the sub-plot, and adding

[1] The Argument would have told him nothing as to its conclusion.
[2] *Neue Untersuchungen zu Shakespeare's 'Mass für Mass'*, pp. 120-4.
[3] There are various sorts of feigned execution in the Æthiopica of Heliodorus and the *Leucippe and Clitophon* of Achilles Tatius, the one already available in English, the other in Latin, Italian and French. See S. L. Wolff, *The Greek Romances in Elizabethan Prose Fiction* (Columbia, 1912).

nothing of consequence, the narrative version could be an abridged redaction of the dramatic, or else of Giraldi's tale re-read; but, in default of conclusive evidence, I am inclined to surmise that events may have taken another course. Whetstone (let us suppose), when he first became acquainted with the *Hecatommithi*, drafted a plot, based on Giraldi's tale, but amplifying it here and there. This draft was fuller than the Argument he prefixed to the printed play, though it corresponded with it in the absence of reference to comic episodes or characters. It was upon this draft that he worked when he had presently to furnish a tale for the fourth day of his *Heptameron*. Eccentricities of narrative manner—failure to mention who the persons are at the first, or even second, occurrence of their names; lapses into the present tense without apparent purpose —these seem to hint at an old plot worked up in haste. There is, on the other hand, nothing to suggest that Whetstone had read the *Hecatommithi* afresh, and some of the amplifications he had put into the play recur in the tale.[1] One, surely, is better handled: both the contrivance of the climax and the expression of what it implies are clarified. The play's knot had been unravelled thus: after his release, Andrugio appears as an outlaw and learns of Promos' downfall,[2] and, in two awkwardly separated soliloquies, summons resolution to discover himself;[3] and the outcome is reported by a messenger: 'Andrugio lives: and Promos is reprivd.' In the tale, Andrugio is moved to attend his enemy's execution, in hermit's disguise; and there, touched by his sister's distress, obtains from King Corvinus the saving clause that Promos might live were Andrugio but *revived*,[4] and discovers himself. Whetstone thereby conveys the idea that the king's will to mercy is liberated by the generous plea of the sister; his power, by the unselfish act of the brother, when for her sake he puts his enemy's safety before his own. Whatever the relationship between the two versions of *Promos and Cassandra*, we cannot (I believe) afford to ignore

[1] There is, for example, the trick of page's disguise for Cassandra.
[2] 2 *Promos and Cassandra*, IV. ii.
[3] Ibid., V. i and iii.
[4] Andrugio pleads: 'If law may possibly be satisfied, Promos' true repentance meriteth pardon.' The King replies: 'He can not live, and the law satisfied, unless (by miracle) Andrugio be revived.' And, sounded further: 'If your prayer can revive the one, my mercy shall acquit the other.'

either: Whetstone's clumsiness admits the possibility that we may find in one what he intended, but failed to say in the other.

That Whetstone had something to say when he was writing his play is surely clear from the design of its sub-plot. This, which is meant to recall Latin comedy and thus to fulfil the other obligation known to Elizabethan theory and (infrequent) practice in comedy, is didactic satire, carefully adjusted to the main plot. Such is the project of a man who believes that he has learnt, at some cost to himself, what is amiss with the world, and is bent on setting it to rights; one, moreover, who has thought about dramatic ends and means, though he lacks practical knowledge of the theatre. Here is no mere succession of droll interludes, but a coherent story of the fortunes of a set of characters who (true to a theory propounded by the dramatist in his dedicatory epistle) never meet the characters of the main plot on the stage nor deal directly with them, but who have been conceived in a certain relation to them. Behind and alongside the main streets of Julio run lanes and alleys and mews,[1] teeming with knaves and their victims. Here Lamia the courtesan reigns until, frightened by her servant Rosko's report that Promos has proclaimed the revival of the old law, she addresses herself to the Deputy's agent and evil genius, Phallax, whose venality is well known, and sells herself to him for her own safety, as Cassandra is forced to sell herself to Promos for her brother's. Meanwhile her maid Dalia traffics with a rich simpleton, and Rosko snaps up what falls. Andrugio's own story is doubled, as in a reflection, by the lamentable fortunes of a train of 'poor rogues' hurried to their death because it is to the advantage of every 'churlish officer' in Julio to multiply offences and punishments. Again, a farcical tail-piece shows a simpleton (not Dalia's victim but another; Whetstone is prodigal of minor characters) forced to buy off the informers who have multiplied under Promos' rule. Examined severally, the persons of this sub-plot seem to be mere clumsy imitations of Plautine types; yet, seen as the design of the play groups them, they compose a crude but vigorous picture of Whetstone's London as he saw it. Indeed, the comic episodes are the most serious part of the play; they were prompted by something that touched experience, and where it touched it hurt. It is to a clown that Whetstone gives

[1] 'Ducke alley, Cocke lane, and Scouldes corner' (2 *Promos and Cassandra*, IV. i).

the pertinent observation that it is most prudent to appeal directly to supreme authority.[1] And it is the sub-plot which asks more insistently than the main plot the question which haunts Whetstone's imagination: who then is fit to be trusted with authority? By piecemeal comparison of similar items we may perhaps discern a resemblance between Corvinus' discourse on justice and a speech on just government by Roilletus' ruler, Prorex.[2] Wider observation of the two plays shows how a topic canvassed by a character in one becomes an issue raised by the whole tenor of the other.

Whetstone's contribution to the development of this story consists in the relation of the events and characters to their background —and by background I mean the whole of the space commanded by the group of characters on which imagination is invited to dwell, and the use to which the dramatist puts it. Promos, Cassandra and Andrugio occupy their share of a parti-coloured world which (as Johnson said, in defending tragi-comedy) corresponds with the world of familiar experience in that it 'partakes of good and evil, joy and sorrow, mingled with endless variety of proportion and innumerable modes of combination', a world 'in which, at the same time, the reveller is hasting to his wine, and the mourner burying his friend'.[3] The problem confronting any writer who attempts this kind of representation is—what the mourner and the reveller have to say to one another when their ways cross. Art must concern itself with this; and so positive and downright an art as Whetstone's cannot well leave it to be inferred.

The next considerable forerunner of *Measure for Measure* is a story in Thomas Lupton's *Siuqila*, which appeared in two parts, one in 1580, the other in 1581[4]—earlier, that is, than the publication, though not necessarily earlier than the composition, of the tale of Promos and Cassandra in Whetstone's *Heptameron*. Since the time of Douce's *Illustrations of Shakespeare*[5] it has been known for an

---

[1] 2 *Promos and Cassandra*, III. ii.
[2] Ibid., I. viii; *Philanira*, Act IV.
[3] *Preface to Shakespeare* (1765), p. xiii.
[4] *Siuqila. Too good, to be true*; and *The Second part and knitting up of the Boke entituled Too good to be true*.
[5] I. 155. J. O. Halliwell-Phillipps added the information that it occurs in the 1581 continuation. (*Memoranda on Shakespeare's Comedy of Measure for Measure*, 1880.)

analogue, but what is of chief interest—the context—has not been enough regarded. *Siuqila*, like its author, is little known; which is understandable, for no one, knowing a little of Lupton and his writings, would desire his better acquaintance. His published works bear the marks of a gross and illiberal mind. Apart from a popular book of nostrums, they are all didactic, and of a particular complexion. Sin and chastisement compose his favourite theme, and he addresses himself to it with appalling relish.

The first part of *Siuqila* suggests an attempt to follow More's *Utopia*, at some distance. The name of the book, and the principal places and persons, are simple anagrams. Siuqila (Aliquis) comes from Ailgna (Anglia) to the frontier of Mauqsun (Nusquam) and there encounters one of its citizens, Omen (Nemo), who will not allow him to enter for fear of the moral infection he may bring. By way of compensation for this denial, he recounts to him the glories of the forbidden country, while poor Siuqila must complement every assertion and anecdote with some confession of the imperfections of his own land. Lupton saw England from the standpoint of a narrow sect. To a vein of anti-papist invective he adds antagonism to the rich and merciless censure of the shiftless poor. Like Whetstone, Lupton speaks primarily for the social class to which he supposes himself to belong, and sees life weighted against it. In Mauqsun, it seems, the law is so framed as to redress this balance: it is grounded, so he alleges, on Christianity and common sense. In practice, this means the identification of sin and crime, with a devising of such punishments, to meet and match all offences, as make the penal code of the *Thousand and One Nights* appear liberal and humane. As for Lupton's Christianity, it consists in self-willed interpretation of certain selected passages from the Bible. The injunction (quoted in the opening[1] and often reiterated), 'Whatsoever you would that men shoulde doe to you, even so do ye to them', is twisted to read: 'Whatsoever, in the darkness of your heart, you would—given the opportunity—have done to others, that shall be done to you.' ('Do as you would be done by'; but not, 'Forgive as you would be forgiven'.) This system is sustained by an army of informers, and a readiness on the part of authority to make information profitable. The simplicity

[1] p. 32.

which Omen claims for it[1] is a simplicity of denial: whereas Whetstone and other reformers had asked that pleasure should be regulated, Lupton asks that it should be forbidden. This simplicity, together with the efficiency of informers, has reduced criminal cases to such proportions that the king can attend to them all himself; thus, there is no court of appeal.

The first part of *Siuqila* ends abruptly, but this is not out of keeping with the clumsiness of the writing; there is nothing to suggest intended continuation. It may, however, have been sufficiently well received[2] to encourage Lupton to continue. Of this second part, only one edition is known; and yet it is the more cunningly framed for entertainment. The two persons of the former dialogue again converse, and again the happy state of Mauqsun is displayed, 'against the envy of less happier lands'. There justice regulates disposal of benefices and land tenure. Omen illustrates at length his thesis that equity in Mauqsun rests firm on the triple foundation of respect for its principles in the hearts of the judges, ferocious severity in punishing all miscarriages of justice, and lavish reward for reporting them. A judge himself may, by disclosing an attempt to bribe him, recover half the sum offered. Some judges, in their zeal, have joined the company of informers. 'There was a Judge with us that feared God, and loved equitie so much, that divers times he would walk in the streates early and late, in unknowne apparel, only to spie pore strangers and Suters, and to enquire of them the cause of their travell and sute.'[3] The King himself has been known to play such a part.[4] It is indeed a favourite device; and it is the group of tales illustrating its use which forms the setting for the story of the monstrous ransom in *Siuqila*. For the poor traveller, seeming to weary of his allotted part, undertakes to show that, even in his own country, justice is sometimes to be found—at the top.

The story belongs to the popular tradition according to which the victims of the unjust judge are husband and wife, and the end calamitous. It is, however, told at uncommon length:[5] an intrigue

---

[1] 'I perceyve you have manye good lawes, and evill kepte: but we have but fewe, and very well kepte'—i.e., enforced (p. 34).
[2] It was to be reprinted in 1584 and 1587.
[3] T. iv. r.   [4] Z. ii. r.   [5] It occupies pp. L. iii. v. to O. iv. v.

is devised to produce the situation in which the husband kills his former friend; the wife discusses the case with the judge at a first interview; when she is recalled and presented with his demand for a sum of money and her surrender, and signifies her unwilling compliance, his instructions are minute and circumstantial. It is these circumstances that supply her with evidence when, upon the news of her husband's death, she tells her tale to the 'Magistrates and the chief Rulers of the Countrey'.[1] (Many of Lupton's stories turn on a question of evidence.) The usual sentence of marriage and execution follows; and the woman is left seemingly well satisfied with her widow's jointure.

Another development of the popular tradition requires particular mention, for the writer, like Lupton, has entered into the circumstances of the tale with some fulness of invention. It is found in the latter part of the *Cinquieme, et dernier volume des nouvels de Bandel*, which was published in 1583 at Lyons, bringing to a close the well-known *Histoires Tragiques*. This work, appearing volume by volume from 1559, had been at the outset a translation of stories from Bandello by Pierre Boisteau and François de Belleforest. The 1583 volume, however, is wholly Belleforest's, and this latter part of it is composed not of translations but of stories for which he takes the sole responsibility.[2] It is grave and monitory in tone, and this particular story, which occupies a substantial share of this part, is explicitly offered as a warning against the disastrous power of lust, with a reference to the history of Uriah the Hittite. True to French narrative tradition, it makes sense: the situation is logically conceived, motive and action are intelligible. The victims are a rash and quarrelsome young soldier, and his wife, who goes in terror of precipitating a fatal brawl; their oppressor is a captain who has from the first schemed to get them into his power. He plays on the young man's weakness, much as Iago plays on Cassio's propensity to quarrel when drunk. Authority is represented by the Marshal, 'Messire Charles de Cossé, Seigneur de Brissac, Gouverneur de Piedmont',[3] celebrated for justice and

[1] O. i. r.
[2] 'Ces Trois Dernieres Histoires sont de l'invention de François de belle Forest...'
[3] Historical names occur in many versions of the story. The namelessness of Lupton's characters is exceptional.

clemency. He has discipline to preserve, and must take care how he proceeds against an officer who, in dealing summarily with a brawl, has committed no technical offence. Thus there is occasion for firmly knit intrigue, for manœuvre and counter-manœuvre, on the part of the three principal characters. The design of wrongdoing and retribution is inexorably traced.

Three subsequent versions, all current in some form before the probable date of *Measure for Measure*, require cursory notice. The first of these shifts the emphasis slightly. Thomas Danett published his version of Commines' history in 1596.[1] In his dedication to Burghley he says that the translation was made some thirty years ago, has circulated since in manuscript among his friends, and has, with their help, been recently enlarged. One substantial addition is a *Supplie* (supplement) for the years 1483 to 1493. It contains this story, framed to illustrate the theme of a favourite's fall: the extortioner suffers punishment because he survives the death of his protector. Thus there is no occasion for the courage, or desperation, which elsewhere impels the victim to obtain justice at whatever cost. The second, a baldly traditional form of the story, appears in Thomas Beard's collection of horrifying tales, *The Theatre of God's Judgements* (1597). It is of no interest. The third, again a plain, harsh tale of oppression brought to light too late for redress but in time for retribution, was told by Simon Goulart, in the first part of his *Histoires Admirables et Memorables de Nostre Temps*, which appeared in Paris in 1600, and a translation of which by Edward Grimeston was to appear in 1607.[2] The victim is a citizen of Como. Authority, in the person of the Duke of Ferrara, intervenes only to punish, and the punishment takes the usual form.[3]

This, I believe, completes the tale of the versions of this painful story which may have been known to Shakespeare when he wrote

[1] *The Historie of Philip de Commines Knight, Lord of Argenton.*
[2] *Admirable and Memorable Histories containing the Wonders of our Time.* Grimeston seems to have translated only this first part, not those which followed in 1601 (II and III), and 1604 (IV). See L. C. Jones, *Simon Goulart* (Geneva, 1917) for the editions of Goulart's work, and G. N. Clark, 'Edward Grimeston' (*English Historical Review*, 1928, xliii. 585–98) for the limited scope of Grimeston's translation.
[3] Goulart was familiar also with a similar story, told by Henri Estienne in his *Apologie pour Hérodote* (Geneva, 1566), in which no mention is made of punishment.

Measure for Measure, and to one or another among the audience when it was first performed. One further *illustration* should however be considered, if only as an analogue. There is a group of plays, not far in date from *Measure for Measure*, in each of which a character of some importance plays a part which has invited comparison with Shakespeare's Vincentio. Hazlitt noticed this, but the course of his immediate argument bore him away from *Measure for Measure*, and (perhaps by reason of his antipathy to this play) he never took occasion to return and follow up the comparison. Of Marston's *Fawn* he remarks (in his *Lectures on the Age of Elizabeth*) that its disguised duke 'may put in a claim to a sort of family likeness to the Duke, in *Measure for Measure*',[1] though he admits that this Hercules of Ferrara 'is only a spy on private follies', and so but distantly related to Vincentio. With *The Fawn* he presently couples *The Malcontent* and its disguised observer, Malevole, arguing that such characters are designed to mediate the theme of the play to us. To Marston's name, Professor W. W. Lawrence in his turn adds Middleton's. He mentions *The Phoenix*,[2] but does not develop the suggestion, and it is the comparison with Marston alone that has attracted attention. Mr. O. J. Campbell associates with *The Malcontent* and *The Fawn*, *Antonio and Mellida*, likening Felice to Shakespeare's Duke.[3]

It is, however, in Middleton's *Phoenix* alone that I find a significant analogy with *Measure for Measure*. Marston's malcontents do indeed 'spy on private follies', and are licensed to comment on them, in Thersites' manner, like parasites tickling those whom they infest. Some of them may, at some juncture, interpret some part of the meaning of the play to us, in their set pieces of declamatory satire—but even here they do not come near the Duke, who is quite devoid of their melancholic humour. Middleton's Phoenix, however, is engaged in an enterprise which bears some resemblance to his, at least in the exposition. The son of an ageing Duke of Ferrara, he has reason to suspect lax administration, and therefore *gives out* that he will travel abroad, the better to lurk in disguise at home and discover hidden abuses. The suggestion that he

---

[1] *Works*, ed. Howe (1930–4), v. 226.
[2] *Shakespeare's Problem Comedies* (New York, 1931), p. 215.
[3] *Shakespeare's Satire* (Oxford, 1943), p. 127.

should leave Ferrara has come from treacherous courtiers, and part of his success consists in the unravelling of a conspiracy among those who have wished him out of the way; part, in his intervention in the affairs of those who (as he had suspected) are hindered of access to justice. By an ingenious trick—he hires himself out to each of the evil-doers in turn—he obtains the information needed for eventual interposition. It is an ugly picture that he sees from his coign of vantage: law hides more fraud and violence, marriage more licence, than were ever to be seen in the disorderly quarters of a city. Every courtier encountered is a traitor, and the chief among them plans to assassinate the old duke, and fasten the guilt on his absent son. This argument fritters itself away in loosely illustrative episodes: scenes exhibiting the litigious man, the venal magistrate and his bullies, the licentious married woman. Nevertheless, the evident intention is analogous with Shakespeare's. Since critical opinion has tended to shift the date of Middleton's play back to 1603,[1] *Phoenix*[2] may well have preceded *Measure for Measure*, and been known to Shakespeare: but its interest derives rather from analogy than from precedence. This mediocre play will show where lay the opportunities, and where the limits, of this old story of the prince incognito setting all to rights:[3] which parts will take the strain and admit development, and which are agreeable only to the taste of a particular age. It may serve to measure what can, and what cannot, be done without the Shakespearian magic.

Two other plays stand in an illustrative relationship to *Measure for Measure*: Davenant's *The Law against Lovers*,[4] and Gildon's *Measure for Measure, or Beauty the Best Advocate*; both being attempts to *improve* it. Pepys saw a performance of *The Law against Lovers* in February of 1662, but it was not printed until the

---

[1] Bullen put it at 1606; E. K. Chambers, 1604; R. C. Bald argues from the condition of the theatres that it belongs to the end of Elizabeth's reign, and from its style that it may be as early as 1602 ('The Chronology of Middleton's Plays', *Modern Language Review*, 1937); Baldwin Maxwell, that the political allusions point to the summer of 1603 ('Middleton's *Phoenix*' in *John Quincy Adams Memorial Studies*, New York, 1948).   [2] 1607. ed. Bullen, *Works*, 1885–6, vol. i.
[3] V. O. Freeburg (*Disguise Plots in Elizabethan Drama*, New York, 1915) mentions the resemblance in plot between *Phoenix* and *Measure for Measure*, but remarks nothing further.
[4] Ed. Maidment and Logan, *Dramatic Works* (Edinburgh, 1872–4), vol. v.

posthumous folio of Davenant's *Works* appeared in 1673. It is a medley composed of parts of *Measure for Measure* (considerably changed), the passages between Beatrice and Benedick from *Much Ado about Nothing* (these again altered) and a conclusion of Davenant's own invention. *Measure for Measure, or Beauty the Best Advocate* appeared in quarto in 1700—anonymously, but the ascription to Charles Gildon has remained unquestioned. Gildon (who owes something to Davenant) abolishes all traces of low life and borrows Purcell's *Dido and Æneas* to fill the vacant spaces. (This, it has been conjectured, may account for the success of his version on the stage.) With the parts of Shakespeare's play that he retains, he takes some trouble. Of these two travesties, his is the more interesting.

II

THE POSITION OCCUPIED BY
MEASURE FOR MEASURE

'There is no great merit in telling how many plays have ghosts in them, and how this ghost is better than that. You must shew how terrour is impressed on the human heart.'

(Johnson, as reported by Boswell, 1769)

WHERE does Shakespeare stand—first, in relation to others who have told the story he tells in *Measure for Measure*; then, in relation to those currents of thought and feeling with which it has now and again been charged?

To his predecessors he may be in debt, directly or indirectly, according as they are indebted to one another. Reckoning backwards from the end of the sixteenth century, we find that the significant figures in the history of this tale amount to five:[1] Roilletus, Giraldi, Whetstone, Lupton, Belleforest. Amongst these, we shall hardly expect a close connection between any writer who makes the man and woman husband and wife, and the end calamitous, and one who makes them brother and sister, and brings about some sort of happy ending. Nevertheless, there must always remain the possibility that either knew, even though he did not choose to follow, the other's version, and that this knowledge will be somewhere reflected. Now, Shakespeare's acquaintance with Whetstone, and *at least* through him with Giraldi's tale, is so evident and so generally accepted that we may surely take it as a fixed point from which to work: through *Promos and Cassandra* he would receive so much of the tale of Epitia as Whetstone himself was able to apprehend and communicate; but by this channel he would not, on my showing, receive anything that is to be found

[1] Assuming that we have not to reckon with a missing intermediary—always a possibility in that age, as the records of lost plays remind us.

only in Giraldi's play; or, in that of Roilletus. Are we to allow for the possibility that he had himself read either of these, or that he knew more of Giraldi's tale, or tales, than Whetstone could tell him?

This poses the old question of Shakespeare's knowledge of other languages besides his own—a question that is not likely ever to be quite resolved. We may, however, start afresh from Professor F. P. Wilson's finding, as to the three languages here involved: Latin, Italian, French—Roilletus' play being extant in Latin and French, Giraldi's play in Italian only, his tale of Epitia in Italian and French.

We shall say . . . that his Latin, small indeed in comparison with Jonson's, was yet sufficient to make him not wholly dependent upon translation. . . . That he read Ovid as well as Golding's Ovid, some Seneca and Virgil as well as English Seneca and Virgil is, I think proved. . . . On these matters there is general agreement. . . . he could and did read in the originals some Terence and Plautus, some Ovid and Virgil; . . . possessing a reading knowledge of Latin all those short-cuts to learning in florilegia and compendia were at his service if he cared to avail himself of them . . . But granted that Shakespeare could read Latin, is there any evidence that he had access to any modern tongue other than his own? Here, I think, there is no general agreement. The evidence that he read Italian depends solely upon the fact that no English versions are known of some of the tales from which he took his plots. For *Cymbeline* did he turn to the *Decameron*, for *Othello* to Cinthio, and for *Measure for Measure* to Cinthio's *novella* and play as well as to George Whetstone's rendering of Cinthio? That an Englishman who can read Latin can make sense of an Italian *novella* has been proved experimentally again and again, but that Shakespeare read at all easily and widely in Italian literature—in Petrarch, Ariosto, and Tasso as well as in the writers of *novelle*—has not, I think, been proved. And as doubtful is the extent of his reading in French literature.[1]

Let me carry this but a little further, before bringing it to bear on the immediate problem. Argument as to Shakespeare's knowledge of languages used to hang on the disputed point, whether it was possible for him to have done what he did without knowing other tongues than his own. The processes of genius being mysterious, we may well believe that a man endowed with it can dispense

[1] F. P. Wilson, 'Shakespeare's Reading' (*Shakespeare Survey* 3, Cambridge, 1950, pp. 14, 15).

with what we call common knowledge—that complex tissue of fact and opinion on which we ourselves depend. But that is no reason for assuming, without substantial proof, that he is wanting in it. To argue so is much like supposing that a craftsman, reputed to have been so skilful that he could do deftly with one hand what other men do clumsily with two, must have been one-handed. If Shakespeare was like other men of his time and place, men whose business brought them acquainted with dwellers in, and visitors to, Elizabethan London, then he shared their inducement to make themselves conversant with other tongues besides their own, for, wanting a knowledge of French, Italian, Spanish, all three, he would be confined to a very narrow room. I think we can hardly realize how different the world must have appeared to Englishmen before sea-faring and commerce had carried our language round it. And opportunity bore some proportion to need. A Londoner could hear French, Flemish or Italian spoken in the Protestant refugee communities, without personal acquaintance amongst them. There were foreign books from English presses or brought home by travellers, and the means of learning to make them out: handbooks of instruction in French and Italian, vocabularies and books offering two or more versions of a work printed in parallel columns—the unready linguist knows how useful these can be. Moreover, Shakespeare himself must have had his full share of that relish for linguistic innovation on which he could evidently count in his audience; and, since this innovation consisted largely in the importation of foreign words, he who had not an ear for these new-comers would be at a loss even in common talk.[1] And there is one further consideration that has been too little regarded: scholars and travellers, from Ben Jonson onwards, have never been able to realize on how small a linguistic capital the rest of us are able to pursue those inquiries to which curiosity prompts us, nor to allow that—whatever else may be beyond our means—we can usually make out a *story* in any language of which we have so much as a smattering.

Let us, then, reckon with the possibility that what was extant in French or Italian may have been within Shakespeare's reach, but

[1] See G. D. Willcock, *Shakespeare as Critic of Language* (Shakespeare Association, 1934).

not admit the probability of his reaching out for books difficult to obtain or to read, in either language. Compared with Whetstone he had just so much more opportunity of acquaintance with these two plays as the time-interval between *Promos and Cassandra* and *Measure for Measure* gives; but he had surely far less incentive to look into them, to penetrate the distasteful rind of an uncongenial dramatic convention, the hard shell of a foreign language[1]—and all for so dry a kernel: a story with which, very likely, he was already familiar on easier terms. Whetstone, when he wrote his play, had been a young man with aspirations after a theory of drama, and without dramatic experience.

Indeed, any argument from accessibility leads towards a position which no one would willingly hold, for it works out like this: Whetstone could not have known *Epitia* and may therefore be credited with enough inventive power for major innovations; Shakespeare could have known it, and therefore is not to be supposed capable of inventing even those circumstances in respect of which *Measure for Measure* comes nearer to *Epitia* than *Promos and Cassandra* had done; yet such circumstances are trifling, within the capacity of the merest artificer to invent, at need.[2]

I believe that we may dismiss the two plays without further concern; but the *Hecatommithi* is another matter altogether. Notwithstanding its much greater dispersion,[3] my claim for it will rest neither on this nor on particular similarities between the fifth tale of the eighth day and *Measure for Measure*, but on something of wider implications. In the *Hecatommithi*, Giraldi tells the tale of the monstrous ransom three several times; and not only is it a favourite story-pattern—it carries the burden of some of his favourite themes. In default of an English translation, the following epitomes of those two versions which have not hitherto been noticed may be useful.

---

[1] The style of Giraldi's play is more formal and difficult than that of his tales. I have read only the original Latin of Roilletus' play, but there seems no reason for supposing the French version to be any less rhetorical and high-pitched.

[2] This must seem a very summary way of dismissing the careful arguments of Albrecht, Budd and Ball, but close and prolonged scrutiny of the particulars has convinced me that they have not the significance claimed for them.

[3] Though the first edition had been printed at Mondovi, those of 1566, 1574, 1580, 1584 and 1593 all issued from the important Venetian presses.

The story occurs twice in the series of stories assigned to the fifth day, of which the ruling subject is: devotion on the part of husband or wife in the teeth of adverse fortune. Within this series, these two form part of a smaller group of similar tales, in each of which the wife rescues the husband from danger by daring, cunning or effrontery.

The second tale of this fifth day is boldly romantic. In the time of Constantine, Viaste governs Constantinople and stands high in the Emperor's favour. He covets Dorothea, wife of Locrino, a prosperous and honourable merchant, who, when Viaste approaches him with dishonourable proposals, lays the case before his wife. She, who seems the stronger spirit, advises him to feign consent; she will undertake to preserve her own honour and his safety. In a long and ably rhetorical argument with Viaste she attempts to change his purpose, but fails. Viaste trumps up a charge against Locrino, and demands the death penalty. The Emperor, though convinced of Locrino's guilt (so skilfully has the charge been framed), will not go beyond the sentence of imprisonment. Viaste vainly tempts first his prisoner, then the prisoner's wife, with the monstrous proposal. From this point onwards, the story develops into a romance of adventure. Locrino's prison is a fortress surrounded by water. But it seems that the ladies of Constantinople were then notable swimmers; and Dorothea swims nightly to the fortress and talks with her husband at a grating. One night the gaoler overhears their talk and, relenting (for he knows his prisoner to be innocent), admits her for a short while. After several such visits he is persuaded to connive at Locrino's escape; and Dorothea contrives their flight from Constantinople. Three years later, Viaste dies, confessing that his accusation was false. Constantine sends word to recall the fugitives, and, after further adventures and escapes, they return to favour and prosperity.

The sixth tale of the same day is, on the other hand, broadly comic in temper. The emphasis falls on the sturdy independence of the husband and wife, and the clemency and placability of the sovereign. A tailor of Ferrara is convicted of theft and condemned to death by a judge who holds office under Alfonso I. He begs for the company of his wife Gratiosa in prison. The judge, well versed in law but a man of vicious character, consents, provided she be willing, and himself interviews her. She is a handsome woman, and tears become her. The judge suggests that after the tailor's death she may well find a better husband. She replies that she wants no better, and pleads that dire necessity alone drove her husband to offend. The judge makes his abominable proposal. Gratiosa forces a way to the Duke's presence and there pleads vigorously and effectually. He conceals her and, sending for his officer of justice, questions him as to the severity of this particular sentence: had he not power to temper the law in these pitiable circumstances? The judge has to admit that the civil code does not impose the death penalty for theft, but maintains that the statutes of the Duke's own city bind him to severity. The Duke rejoins: 'What about the tailor's wife?'—and produces her, voluble and accusing; and the judge is dumbfounded. The Duke decrees that, in recompense for his wife's merit, the tailor shall be pardoned, and what he has stolen shall be made good out of the judge's property; the judge is to lose his life. The judge's friends appeal for mercy, pleading his youth and the woman's beauty; but the Duke retorts that a magistrate should be superior to common frailty. A young man of his court ventures the pleasantry that even the old and wise are not always proof against temptation—he himself might have succumbed if he had seen her in tears and not in a temper. The Duke relents, and the judge's friends obtain his pardon.

Set the three tales I have summarised—they may for convenience be called the tales of Epitia, Dorothea and Gratiosa—side by side, and it will surely appear that Giraldi was bent on ending this story happily, and varied the means in accord with current moral sentiment: where the woman is unmarried, any wrong done her is repaired by marriage;[1] where she is, as in traditional versions, the wife of the condemned man, means must be devised for keeping her person inviolate. Comparison, moreover, suggests another significant resemblance amongst the three: a verdict (which varies from flagrantly unjust to excessively severe) is wisely and happily overruled in each by higher authority. Giraldi's ideal sovereign is

[1] Puritan moralists of Shakespeare's age did not subscribe to this opinion. See, for example, the context of this story in Thomas Beard's *Theatre of God's Judgements*.

one who conceives it within his power and his duty to temper the law with mercy; and, even with due allowance for the obvious usefulness of such a personage in tragi-comedy, and the likelihood of flattery when he appears in tales dedicated to members of a ruling house, this figure still looks to me emblematical. He is to be seen also in other tales of the fifth day, and of this same group: the fourth, in which a woman rescues her husband from prison by changing clothes with him, is condemned to suffer in his stead, and, when he gives himself up, to suffer with him; and the fifth, in which again a wife rescues her husband from prison by a stratagem involving change of dress, and sentence of death is delivered by the magistrate in charge. In both, this magistrate's sentence is overruled by Francis of Savoy: in one, friends of the imperilled couple hold up the execution until an appeal can reach the king; in the other, the two lie perdu until their pardon is obtained from him, and the magistrate put out of office.

This idea of royal clemency is exemplified in another and graver tale, and there associated with one of Giraldi's favourite themes: generosity to a fallen enemy. In the sixth tale of the sixth day, Livia, a widow devoted to an only son, heroically pleads for the life of the man who has killed that son in a brawl and unwittingly taken refuge in her house. The judge, represented as a stickler for the law, will not be moved; but she addresses herself to the highest authority of all, because 'la Divina Bontà hà data a voi aut[t]orità sopra le leggi, & arbitri di mitigar l'asprezza loro'. To her, as to Epitia, the thing she asks is granted, in recognition of her magnanimity: 'Vinca Donna la tua cortesia la severa auttorità delle leggi'.

Surely anyone glancing through the *Hecatommithi* and reading these among other tales would receive certain impressions: first, that this story was capable of being brought, by a variety of means, to the happy ending proper to tragi-comedy; a conclusion, that is, in which it appears that no irreparable wrong has been done or suffered.[1] With this, two complementary ideas of mercy would remain in the reader's mind: of the inclination to pardon which is to be looked for in the man of highest authority; of the capacity to forgive which may be called forth, even in one much injured, by

[1] Ideas as to what sort of wrong is irreparable will vary with time and place.

reversal of fortune, the abject helplessness of a former enemy and oppressor. Are we to suppose Shakespeare such a reader? Given a single assumption—and it is one very commonly held—this is at least a likely supposition: failing the discovery of a separate publication (in any language) of the story of Desdemona and the Moor, which is Giraldi's seventh tale for the third day, we must assume that Shakespeare found it in the *Hecatommithi*—and he would be a dull spirit who, having read one of these tales, should read no further. May we not then suppose that (in the course, perhaps, of a year which saw the first performance of *Measure for Measure* and *Othello*) he found in this same book the tale of Epitia, and those tales of the fifth day which seem to be variations on that very theme? Of Shakespeare's reading in books known to have been favourites with him, Professor F. P. Wilson says: 'The evidence suggests that when a theme took possession of his mind, especially a theme with a long tradition behind it, he read widely—not laboriously, but with a darting intelligence, which quickened his invention.'[1] There is, I believe, nothing inherently improbable in the notion of Shakespeare ranging, with easier, more cursory attention, through the *Hecatommithi*.

As we reach *Siuqila*, in this interrogation of *Measure for Measure*'s principal antecedents, even the faint light of probability flickers. The story itself, belonging to that tradition from which Giraldi, Whetstone and Shakespeare alike depart, has little to connect it with any of their versions—unless we allow that the circumstantial contrivance, out of the judge's own means of security, of the evidence by which he is destroyed may have quickened Shakespeare's interest in the practical problem of furnishing *stage proofs*. But it is the story's context for which I claim attention: that group of neighbouring tales whose central figure is an indefatigably inquisitive ruler. Here Lupton, taking that creature of popular imagination, the prince who benevolently intermeddles in private lives, develops a busy concern with the various sorts of subterfuge proper to the part. Thus in Ailgna, where the story itself is set, the burden of proof falls on the victim of oppression; but in Mauqsun, the setting of many neighbouring tales, authority takes measures to ascertain the truth in good time, to thwart the oppressor—and

[1] 'Shakespeare's Reading' (*Shakespeare Survey*, 3, 1950), p. 18.

punish him for what he would have done. If *Siuqila* indeed lingered in Shakespeare's imagination, it must have owed its presence there to that strangely retentive force of disgust, which would not release Fielding until he had given his own version of Pamela's history.

With Belleforest, the light goes out; for, though Shakespeare may well have known and used certain of the *Histoires Tragiques* elsewhere,[1] he would have found these in earlier volumes than that of 1583. There seems nothing to connect him with those three tales in the second part of the 1583 volume which are distinguished as Belleforest's own.[2] I propose therefore to regard Belleforest's version of the story as a mere analogue, worth remembering for the sake of the significant contrast which it here and there affords with the versions of Giraldi, Whetstone and Shakespeare.

If these relationships which I have characterized as probable should ever be found susceptible of proof; or if the sum of my conjectures should in the meanwhile be accepted as a working hypothesis—what should we stand to gain? The authority required to lay a ghost, a whispering spirit, always ready to insinuate that Shakespeare, when he wrote *Measure for Measure*, was handling carelessly a story unfit for his art; that, under some pressure (probably discreditable), he thrust upon this ugly tale an incongruous happy ending—saving himself the trouble of fresh invention by forced levy upon a worthless old play. It may seem to those who share the recent veneration for *Measure for Measure* that this is all an old story, better forgotten. Nothing so strongly felt as this has been felt is effaced merely by another mode of feeling. Its dismissal may not be final: I believe that until we give it the whole benefit of the doubt, stating it afresh in our own best terms, we shall never obtain that command by which alone a house is rid of such visitants.

Let me begin with the moderate view, the view of temperate people who are ready to enjoy what they find enjoyable in the play—but are not prepared to face all the issues raised by their partial acceptance of its implications. Shakespeare, they tell us,

---

[1] Belleforest's versions of Bandello have been canvassed as sources for *Much Ado* and *Twelfth Night*; of Saxo Grammaticus, for *Hamlet*.

[2] I have mentioned a resemblance between the captain's treatment of the husband and Iago's treatment of Cassio—a particular in which *Othello* diverges from Giraldi's story; but it is too tenuous to bear the weight of argument.

took a harsh tale and softened it. But how? By preserving the woman from violation—that is, he found someone to suffer in her place. And if this should seem hardly sufficient we may be assured that, since her substitute is already betrothed to the judge, and betrothal had then a legal validity whose force we have now forgotten, all is indeed well. This contention[1] has already been met[2] by the objection that the law alone would be appeased by this solution of the difficulty, religious belief and moral sentiment remaining unsatisfied. When we remember what Claudio, as well as his sister, has to say on the anticipation of marriage by a betrothed couple, it certainly seems that here is an anomaly; and, where moral sentiment and law are at variance, the dramatist who should prefer to satisfy the law would, even now, be choosing strangely; while, in that age at least, religion had to be reckoned with. As to that other 'softening'—a more sparing use of the property head than was to be looked for in that remote, terrible Elizabethan theatre—how would it affect the audience for whom the play was intended? Did they indeed react to feigned death as we do? If they really cared that Isabel should not see, on or off the stage, the head which she is to suppose her brother's, why did not Shakespeare spare Imogen an equally horrible experience? The faked executions in popular narrative of that age[3] were witnessed by characters nearly concerned; otherwise they would have been pointless, the deception being designed for these very people.

It may be worth while to follow to their logical conclusion the implications of this proposition—that a harsh tale may be softened by the substitution of a less interesting victim for one in whose sufferings we have come to feel concern. Shakespeare (it will then appear) used this device three times: on behalf of Claudio, Isabel and Barnardine—and only the first of these had been suggested by his known source. Pursuing this path, we find ourselves confronted with a dramatist of unflagging professional competence, who has been urged to repeat his recent success in romantic comedy,

---

[1] It was first advanced by W. W. Lawrence, in *Shakespeare's Problem Comedies* (Chapter iii); and, as to the validity of Elizabethan betrothal in the eyes of the law, has been fully substantiated and accepted.

[2] See D. P. Harding, 'Elizabethan Betrothals and *Measure for Measure*' (*Journal of English and Germanic Philology*, April 1950). This argument will be considered in the analysis of the play; see pp. 119-20 below.   [3] E.g., in Sidney's *Arcadia*.

and is now engaged in turning over in his mind, with enforced patience, the possibilities of this familiar tale—already fashioned, by Whetstone's good nature, into something that might once have passed for tragi-comedy, but was not yet fit for the taste of the new court. Unconcernedly he observes that, by doubling that old substitution trick—the very staple of romance, whether popular or courtly—he will be able to meet the utmost demand that can be made on him. The brother has already been saved from the peril that threatened him; why not the sister, and by similar means? Let a substitute for her too be invented; and, in the very act of calling this other woman into being, the harassed dramatist finds himself relieved of the duty of providing for her: she will of course marry the judge. And here he may be supposed to feel weariness, and disgust itself, evaporating in the very glow of success, or at least in the exercise of his own ingenuity; and, warming to his work, will ask himself: 'But why stop here? Is no provision to be made for that other humble, serviceable character—the prisoner whose head the kindly gaoler took the liberty of removing, for the benefit of the condemned man? Why not yet another substitute, for *his* benefit? A thoughtless audience cannot have too much of a happy ending.' —There, in plain terms, however ludicrously framed, is Raleigh's proposition (less than half jest): that if Shakespeare had been asked for a comedy when he was in no mood for writing one, he would not have answered, 'Can't you see that I am in my tragic period?' —he would have delivered *Measure for Measure*.[1] And there is the logical outcome of supposing that Shakespeare had no more to do in this business than to find his way by the smoothest possible passage to the happiest possible ending.

Nevertheless, the logical conclusion is not always the right point from which to examine a supposition; fairness sometimes requires that we should go back and frame the argument afresh in terms for which we are prepared to accept responsibility. Thus, if it were granted that the prevailing tone of *Measure for Measure* is romantic, it might be argued that romance obeys one sole law—to please; that any kind of art which serves no other end than this is doomed to exhaust itself in an effort to outdo itself, and sooner or later 'dies in his own too much'. More particularly, it might be urged

[1] Walter Raleigh, *Shakespeare* (1907), p. 131.

that romance is compelled to ripen, and rot, in a certain manner, which may be thus predicted: whereas most stories are stories of a choice to be made and its outcome, the simplest sort of romantic story presents a choice between good and bad; its hero takes at the outset the bad way—otherwise there would have been no story—but it is plainly to be understood that he is impelled to take it by something for which he will not ultimately be held to account. The world of this kind of romance obeys a rule of ideal equity, and, where a man is not (according to its conventions) to blame for what he has done, we may be sure that some favourable chance will intervene between the act and its natural consequence. This simple species is bound by the law of its own nature presently to give place to one less simple. Contrasts are heightened: on the one hand the act and the expected consequence worsen; on the other, we are asked to rate ever higher the worth of the man who performs the act, and to delight ever more in the felicity at which he somehow or other arrives. Soon, romance finds itself obliged to invade the realm of tragedy: the initial choice affords no good prospect, only alternatives of ill; the intervention by which sympathetic characters are rescued from the proper consequences of their own decisions calls for bold disregard of probability; there is a general agreement to forget the given conditions of the original situation and accept a close which, as it becomes more assured, assumes an air of uncompromising formality.

Is this indeed the phase, in the development of romantic drama, to which *Measure for Measure* belongs? Did the taste of the audience, at the Christmas revels of the new court, demand of the dramatist that he should frame a situation from which a tragic issue was to be expected, and then exploit his power in bending the course of the play away from tragedy? Were the conventional improbabilities of romantic comedy no longer good enough for them? Questions of this sort used to be asked concerning Shakespeare's last plays. For answer, critics pointed to the ideas with which he had charged these romances and fairy tales. Such an answer, if it can be supported, is sufficient. The plain man in the picture gallery trudges stubbornly past the figure of Herodias' daughter holding aloft the head of John the Baptist, and has no mind to stand and gaze for so long as the connoisseur can expatiate on the excellence of the workmanship. Nor will he be placated with the promise that, in the next representation of the subject to meet his eyes, what he dreads to see will be concealed from view. Tell him that it is to be *softened*—say, by disposal of drapery—and he may well reply that this makes matters worse. (Statement is indeed more endurable than suggestion enforced by recollection.) Nevertheless, he should in fairness concede: 'If you can make me understand that it means something, I will look afresh.'

The belief that *Measure for Measure* 'means something', though it is comparatively young[1] (and the claim to esoteric meaning still younger), seems to have outgrown the need for defence. Since the publication of Professor Wilson Knight's *The Wheel of Fire*[2] and R. W. Chambers's *The Jacobean Shakespeare and 'Measure for Measure'*,[3] there have been many to agree (and who that heard him would not wish to agree with R. W. Chambers?) in reading the play as a Christian parable.[4] Here, then, is authority to refute the insinuation that, in *Measure for Measure*, Shakespeare mis-spent himself in saying something that amounts to nothing. Why not accept the assurance that no charge of theatrical opportunism can lie against this play—and be content?

Unhappily, I consider that every one of these expositions, however persuasive, leaves something out of the reckoning; and that, if

[1] Pater's interpretation, in *Fortnightly*, 1874 (*Appreciations*, 1889), announces the theme.

[2] Oxford, 1930; London, 1949.

[3] Originally delivered as the Annual Shakespeare Lecture of the British Academy for 1937.

[4] The influence of this interpretation cannot be measured without taking into account passages on the play in many general studies of Shakespeare, but representative articles devoted to it may be cited: M. C. Bradbrook, 'Authority, Truth and Justice in *Measure for Measure*' (*Review of English Studies*, October 1941). See also the same writer's 'Shakespeare and the Use of Disguise in Elizabethan Drama' (*Essays in Criticism*, April 1952). F. R. Leavis, 'The Greatness of *Measure for Measure*' (*Scrutiny*, January 1942; and *The Common Pursuit*, 1952). D. A. Traversi, '*Measure for Measure*' (*Scrutiny*, Summer 1942). W. M. T. Dodds, 'The Character of Angelo in *Measure for Measure*' (*Modern Language Review*, July 1946). R. W. Battenhouse, '*Measure for Measure* and Christian Doctrine of the Atonement' (*Publications of the Modern Language Association of America*, December 1946). J. C. Maxwell, '*Measure for Measure*, A Footnote to Recent Criticism' (*Downside Review*, 1947). This body of criticism has left a deep impression on recent productions of the play. An attempt to sum up recent argument has been made by R. M. Smith ('Interpretations of *Measure for Measure*', *Shakespeare Quarterly*, October 1950).

we look in the direction of the thing omitted, we shall presently discover an unresolved difficulty. Can we afford, for example, to dwell on the Christian sanction for the forgiveness of Angelo, while ignoring Giraldi's preoccupation with this very theme? How, if we find *his* treatment of it to be grounded elsewhere than in Christianity? Can a claim of such far-reaching implications rest securely on any plea—or even any number of pleas—limited in scope? Sooner or later, it will surely ask to be examined on a scale beyond the proper aim of lecture, article or chapter. Year after year I see the plain man trudge past, unconciliated. Defence that does not satisfy will bring you to a region hardly to be distinguished from that to which attack sends you—or distinguishable from it only by the greater density of its shadows.

Mr. Empson,[1] for example, seems to be cramped by the constricted space in which he has chosen to raise large issues, like a performer forced to turn in too small a circle. Thus, passages in which he patiently examines significant recurrence of word and phrase must alternate with others which appear to depend on impatiently reached conclusions, if the sum of what he would have the reader accept is to be conveyed within the limits of a chapter.

The progress to which I would invite the reader will be slow. We must be free to travel alongside the play,[2] taking it scene by scene, passage by passage, or even line by line, using, when the dialogue seems intricate or obscure, the leisurely device of paraphrase. We must have liberty for make-believe—on which, indeed, criticism is more dependent than we are usually willing to admit: we must bring into use that ideal theatre of the imagination which will allow the pace of a performance to be controlled, varied even from sentence to sentence, and which further permits the producer-auditor to choose his own pauses, and perhaps to cry a halt while he looks backwards over the way he has come.

[1] W. Empson, *The Structure of Complex Words* (1951), Chapter xii.
[2] See the recommendation of Dr. Dover Wilson in *The Fortunes of Falstaff* (Cambridge, 1945), p. 3.

III

THE PLAY CONSIDERED

I. The Case

'What astonishes me is, Shakespeare: when I look into him it is not a Book, but People talking all round me.'
(Edward Fitzgerald, Letter to Mrs. Cowell)

THE ascertainable circumstances of *Measure for Measure* are few indeed. The first extant mention is an entry in the Account Book of the Revels Office, showing that it was performed at Court on 26 December 1604, as one of a series of Christmas entertainments. Since the new sovereign would sometimes command performances of plays which had not been tried out in the public theatre, nothing forbids us to suppose this its first appearance. In default of any evidence to the contrary, I shall refer to this audience of 1604 as the play's original audience. 'There is no other known mention of a performance of this play before the Restoration,'[1] and no known printed text earlier than the Folio.

This single text on which we have to rely has had many hard things said of it since Johnson declared: 'There is perhaps not one of Shakespeare's plays more darkened than this by the peculiarities of its Authour, and the unskilfulness of its Editors, by distortions of phrase, or negligence of transcription.'[2] There *are* disquieting symptoms; but not, I believe, so many nor so grave as we have come to suppose: we are, as we sit down to it, in the position of a patient on whom every successive doctor has pronounced a fresh interdict: we starve, because everything on the table has been forbidden us. Some difficulties can be explained, and some explained away; some, rightly considered, cancel one another out. We may

---

[1] New Cambridge Shakespeare, p. 160.
[2] Head-note to the play in his edition.

eventually find that indubitable textual corruption can be confined to particular passages, and there dealt with piecemeal.

Sir Edmund Chambers gives a by no means hopeless account of the text.[1] Sir Walter Greg likens it to that of *All's Well that Ends Well*, which he believes to be, though faulty, based on the dramatist's own manuscript.[2] He points out, in *Measure for Measure*, the scanty stage directions, the traces of cuts, and the contradictory time scheme, and concludes:

Careless composition has perhaps been made worse by subsequent patching ... I should imagine that a good deal of tidying up of which we know nothing may have been done in preparing the prompt-book. Scribal peculiarities point to a manuscript by Crane, but I think it must have been rather carelessly made from foul papers that had been a good deal altered.[3]

Here is a sobering but not altogether discouraging prospect: it is like being offered hard work with the hope of a livelihood.

I shall require liberty to challenge from time to time not only stage directions but also act- and scene-division. Professor F. P. Wilson (who first suggested Crane's responsibility for the copy of *Measure for Measure* used in the Folio) observes that Crane was careful to divide his transcripts into acts and scenes where this was not already done.[4] I plead that it was not done throughout the foul papers on which he had here to work and that the divisions, though generally systematic and consistent, lack authority and deserve brief notice now.

Scene-division is used for either of two purposes: to indicate lapse of time or change of place, as in modern usage; or to mark the point at which one set of characters retires from the stage and another takes its place. The first kind has, of course, been accepted by editors, but the second has not been so consistently treated. Thus, in Act I, the Folio makes a scene-division within what now

---

[1] *William Shakespeare* (Oxford, 1930), i, 454–7. To the particulars of this account I shall, of course, revert throughout this chapter.

[2] '... an author's manuscript, but some of the directions suggest expansion by a literary editor.... The most likely explanation of the state of the text is perhaps that the author's foul papers were first annotated by the book-keeper and then transcribed by a rather careless literary copyist.' W. W. Greg, *The Editorial Problem in Shakespeare* (Oxford, 1942), p. 146. [3] Ibid., p. 146.

[4] F. P. Wilson, 'Ralph Crane, Scrivener to the King's Players' (*The Library*, September 1926), pp. 211, 212.

appears as Scene ii—that is, at l. 119 (Pompey's exit). In Act IV, it makes a scene-division which has (with no more reason) been accepted, giving us Scenes ii and iii, and separating the withdrawal of the Duke and Provost from the appearance of Pompey.[1] At neither of these points, however, can I find any occasion to suppose change of place or lapse of time. In I. ii., Pompey's announcement of the persons who are to succeed him on the stage forbids the supposition. In IV. ii—iii, there is a natural transition from the Duke's observation that dawn is breaking to Pompey's entry—of which the main purpose is to indicate that the prison is waking to another day. Consistency asks, therefore, that neither of these divisions should be observed on the stage, nor in a text otherwise divided according to modern usage.

In Act III, on the other hand, the Folio makes no division; whereas modern editors mark one at l. 280 (Isabel's exit). Here again the Folio's practice is consistent; the scribe abiding by his own principles—for, though some of the persons are changed,[2] yet the stage has not been vacated: the Duke remains. Here, I see good reason for accepting the Folio's intimation of continuity; observing only that, whereas the action seems hitherto to have fluctuated between inner and outer stage, throughout the remainder of Act III the outer stage will apparently be in constant use.[3]

So far, then, the Folio's scene-division has been workmanlike, while its act-division has raised no difficulties. In that awkward passage from Act IV to Act V, however, both may fairly be called in question. Johnson wished that the act-division might follow upon the conclusion of IV. iv,[4] and certainly a night elapses between the parting here of Angelo and Escalus, and the meeting of Isabel and Mariana with Peter in IV. vi. Where, if anywhere, to put IV. v. with its peculiar difficulties is a question that may never be answered. What is clear is the unbroken continuity from the close of this perplexing scene to the end of the play: no time interval can separate Peter's announcement 'The Duke is ent'ring' from the

---

[1] The New Cambridge Shakespeare indicates no change of place, and appears to keep the traditional scene division for convenience of reference merely.

[2] Isabel withdraws; Elbow, Pompey and Officers enter.

[3] See below, pp. 90-1.

[4] Foot-note to the end of this scene, IV. xii in his edition.

Duke's entrance. Thus, the Folio's division here can stand for nothing more than the clearing of the stage when the women are hurried off.[1] It will be seen therefore that neither act- nor scene-division, as these have become customary in modern editions, is to be accepted unreservedly.

The play's *exposition* occupies the first five scenes, according to the Folio division; the whole of the first act, alike in that and modern editions. By the time this passage has been played out, we have made the acquaintance of the principal persons of the traditional story, besides some new-comers. Moreover, we may be said to know our way about the fabulous 'Vienna' they inhabit.

I do not find in this first act traces of such disorder as to argue the thorough-going corruption that has been suspected;[2] rather, a sprinkling of those faults that are to be met, irregularly concentrated, throughout the whole text, together with some signs of haste not difficult to account for. It is evident from the first that the dramatist is working on a large scale, if only for this reason: his theme is so conceived that part of its import must be conveyed to us through a representation of the world in which the story is set. Whether or no *Vienna* stands for London, as Whetstone's Julio seems to do, it is certainly no mere unmeaning, conventional background. It must be reckoned with, as a place that has its own climate.

The atmosphere of the tragi-comedies which intersperse the *Hecatommithi* had been, as nearly as possible, constant: names of cities might be mentioned, but they carried no associations beyond what the circumstances of the several stories required; the persons stood forth with the large dignity of figures in contemporary Italian painting, and against much the same formal and ideal background. Belleforest, in the ageless tradition of the French novel, had given just so much atmosphere as was needed to make the situation appear in three dimensions; as though anything more would have been a source of confusion. Whetstone, characteristically English, had not only atmosphere, but weather—too much weather for his limited powers of representation. It is difficult to

---

[1] The implications of these scene-divisions will be considered as they are reached in the analysis of the play.
[2] See New Cambridge Shakespeare and New Temple Shakespeare.

see people or things through the driving rain and mist, the tumbling lights and shadows, which play upon his landscape. Shakespeare's stage is similarly crowded with people who have lives of their own, but his characters are presently subdued to the common concernment thrust upon them by the situation. Such a composition as this asks for the energetic expenditure of considerable resources; for rapid development, an impatience both of petty economies and niceties of circumstantial explanation.

The first scene of all draws a little apart from the remainder of the exposition, almost as a prologue might do. Let me have leave to play the producer awhile, in that ideal theatre of the imagination where any proposed interpretation of a play must be put to the test. In some modern productions, the Duke is discovered sitting in state, with court and council about him.[1] The dialogue gives no warrant for this; the Folio stage direction, no more than is implied in the mention of 'Lords', and even this is open to challenge. Suppose the Duke to enter so obviously dressed for travel that it is not unnatural to imagine the groom walking his horse up and down hard by. Let him come attended by Escalus, and followed, at a discreet distance, by some humbler personal attendant —the one who will be needed to fetch Angelo.[2] Recall the abrupt valedictory speech; the references to a plan of departure evidently known to the interlocutors, the swift summoning and entry of Angelo, as though some business were in train and he, perhaps, already commanded to be at hand. Surely all this takes place at the very moment of parting, in privacy, perhaps even in secrecy? Hence the references to haste, the suggestion of irregular procedure, the dismay of Escalus and Angelo when even *their* further attendance is forbidden, and Angelo's subdued protest at the precipitancy of his appointment. At least it may be claimed that the opening gains sensibly in spring and impact, if thus presented.—A drowsy, afternoon session of the privy council, none but Escalus making any reply to the sovereign's observations—which include an inquiry as to Angelo's capacity, most improper for the occasion —could there be a more unpropitious opening for this, or any

---

[1] Cf. stage direction in New Cambridge Shakespeare: 'The council-chamber in the Duke's palace at Vienna. Escalus and other councillors seated at a table: the Duke in his chair of state: two attendants with partisans at the door.'   [2] ll. 15, 16.

play? But a hurried transaction between the Duke, speaking with a strong undercurrent of excitement, and the two men in whom he professes to repose confidence—this wakes expectation, and turns it in the right direction.[1]

The Duke's business is to delegate authority, and he must do this in such a way as to release a current of curiosity. In the absence of witnesses, he delivers a written commission to each of his deputies[2]—in oddly contrasting terms. Escalus is praised for sagacity, and for the knowledge of law, custom and human nature proper to an experienced magistrate, and then given, as it were, sealed orders—

>From which, we would not have you warpe.[3]

Angelo is admonished as one whose qualities, unless they be forcibly put to employment, may remain unused and unknown; but to him is delivered the Duke's own power to amend the law he is to administer—*carte blanche*. This is surely enigmatic behaviour. In three several passages within this one short scene, the peculiar scope of Angelo's commission is made clear. First, the Duke informs Escalus of its terms:

> We have with speciall soule
> Elected him our absence to supply;
> Lent him our terror, drest him with our love,
> And given his Deputation all the Organs
> Of our owne powre.[4]

This is confirmed and heightened in the announcement to Angelo himself:

> In our remove, be thou at full, our selfe:
> Mortallitie and Mercie in *Vienna*
> Live in thy tongue, and heart—[5]

but not within the competence of Escalus. And when Angelo, his

---

[1] It explains, moreover, a curious allusion by Lucio, at III. ii. 99. When he and the Friar have been angling for one another's guesses, as to the absent Duke's whereabouts, he caps the exchange with this comment: 'It was a mad fantasticall tricke of him to steale from the State, and usurpe the beggerie hee was never borne to.' For a duke to have taken leave in this manner is mere beggary—that is, a condition below that of a private gentleman—in Lucio's estimation.

[2] These documents, with the cryptic references to their contents, would surely be out of place in full council.   [3] I. i. 15.   [4] I. i. 18.   [5] I. i. 44.

entreaty for a period of probation silenced, still pleads for time, he is assured:

> Your scope is as mine owne,
> So to inforce, or qualifie the Lawes
> As to your soule seemes good.[1]

This insistence on the signal scope of his powers would be likely to carry to a contemporary audience a certain train of associations. They would be familiar with the idea that it is within the competence of the higher officers of the law to temper the rigour of that very penal code which their subordinates are bound to enforce.[2]

The next part of the exposition[3] shows how Vienna at large reacts to the new situation—much as the opening of *Romeo and Juliet* shows us how Verona at large reacts to any fresh crisis in the feud between Montagues and Capulets; and, as there so here, the general impression is presently brought into focus, that we may see its relevance to a particular case. The means to this end, in *Measure for Measure*, are the vibrations set up by a new proclamation. Whetstone's play had opened with an affair of this sort—Promos ceremoniously reading out his new commission;[4] but Shakespeare, with characteristic economy,[5] intimates that the provisions of Angelo's proclamation are generally known, and leaves us to infer them, piecemeal, as need arises. Emphasis thus falls on the term *proclamation*, and to understand this we must take into account the associations it had been gathering throughout two reigns.[6] Under Henry VIII, royal proclamations had for a while obtained statutory force; under Elizabeth, attempts at legislation by their means commonly provoked protest. The question was to

---

[1] I. i. 65.
[2] See, for example, Lodowick Bryskett's *Discourse of Civill Life* (1606, but probably composed 1586), p. 249. Bryskett's *Discourse* reproduces part of Giraldi's *Dialoghi della vita Civile*, together with other matter, original and derived.   [3] I. ii.
[4] The 'commission' itself is not in the printed text, but a stage direction enjoins the reading aloud.
[5] Compare the avoidance of any explicit statement as to the ground of the quarrel in the Temple Garden (1 *Henry VI*, II. iv.) noticed by Dr. Dover Wilson, Introduction to 3 *Henry VI* (New Cambridge Shakespeare), p. xiii.
[6] See *A Bibliography of Royal Proclamations of the Tudor and Stuart Sovereigns, with an historical essay on their origin and use*, by Robert Steele, 1910; also G. W. Keeton, *Shakespeare and his Legal Problems* (1930).

come to a head under James, in the crisis of 1610, when Coke and his fellow justices declared that 'the King could not, by proclamation, create any new offence, or alter the law of the land; but he might draw attention to existing law, and if a subject disobeyed, the fact that he had ignored the proclamation might be a ground for increasing the punishment'.[1] After this, the use of royal proclamations abated for a while.

Thus, Angelo's first official act, of which the rumour runs through Vienna, would be directly associated with vexatious recollections—so vexatious, that it is surprising to find them recalled in a court play; but, at that court of 1604, they might be taken as referring to a former dispensation: satire might be seen pointing to the successive endeavours under Tudor rule to devise legislation for the regulating of manners, and even appetites, by exhortation and threat.[2] More than one of Elizabeth's proclamations, enjoining some course of behaviour 'on pain of death'—a penalty not enforceable—may have occasioned a mood about equally compounded of irritable uncertainty and dismay. And this I take to be the mood of Vienna when news of Angelo's proclamation gets abroad.

These 204 lines, then, may be taken as showing the impact of Angelo's rule upon Vienna. The editors of the New Cambridge Shakespeare, however, find here such discrepancies as lead them to suspect the intervention of a botcher; and this is a suspicion that cannot wait upon a general survey of the text but must be considered forthwith.

This is how Dr. Dover Wilson states his objection:

Dramatically (he says) I. ii. 1–111 falls into three sections: (*a*) The sorry fooling between Lucio and his two gentlemen, mostly turning upon the unsavoury topic of venereal disease (1–57). In this section there is great confusion in regard to the distribution of parts.... (*b*) A brief dialogue, in much the same style, between Mistress Overdone and the three men (58–79). In the course of this she tells them that Claudio has been arrested 'for getting Madam Julietta with child', and that he will be beheaded within three days, upon which the First Gentleman

---

[1] Keeton, op. cit., p. 34.

[2] The bold treatment of the proclamation in *Henry VIII* (I. iii. 17–48) suggests that, even so soon after the crisis of 1610, the dramatist was safe, provided his aim appeared to be a characteristic piece of Tudor legislation.

comments that her story agrees well 'with the proclamation'. (c) The dialogue between Overdone and Pompey (80–111). Here we find not only a different style ... but [also the intimation] that, in spite of what has gone before, Overdone is completely ignorant of the cause of Claudio's arrest and has never even heard of the proclamation! Clearly section (c) does not belong to the same stratum of the text as sections (a) and (b), and was presumably written on a different occasion and possibly by another hand.[1]

And in his notes on the remainder of the scene Dr. Dover Wilson further contends that there is a similar discrepancy between Lucio's 'ignorance of the circumstances of Claudio's arrest' and the opportunity he has had of learning them from Mrs. Overdone.

This seems a strong case; but its force is sensibly diminished if we consider that at its very base lies a single assumption: it has been assumed that when Pompey tells Mrs. Overdone

> Yonder man is carried to prison,[2]

and hints at his offence, he refers to Claudio, and that Claudio is then within Mrs. Overdone's range of vision. Now, this is by no means certain. A time-discrepancy is at once apparent: it is not until some while afterwards that we see Claudio on his long-drawn-out progress towards the prison—to which, on this showing, he has already been carried; but indications of time are not, in this play, so clear and exact that a single disagreement amongst them will bear much weight. I do not, however, find it necessary to suppose that 'yonder man' is Claudio: Elizabethan dramatic technique allows of ample illustration, by the introduction of persons unknown to the story—when Whetstone wishes to illustrate conditions in Julio, he expends two scenes in presenting the case of six nameless prisoners, led about the streets to their death

> ... for breach of lawes.
> For murder some, for theeverie some, and some for little cause.[3]

Some such episode as this may have been part of Shakespeare's original design, or hovered in his mind while that design was

---

[1] New Cambridge Shakespeare, p. 99. I think it may be assumed that, if the major discrepancies are not proven, the argument from faulty distribution of parts, and from J.D.W.'s impression of variations in style, will not stand; for the former is explicable in foul papers, and the latter is matter of opinion.   [2] I. ii. 87.
[3] 1 *Promos and Cassandra*, II. ix. (should be vii). See also the preceding scene.

forming; if he relinquished it, he must have forgotten to remove its traces. On this supposition, the man of whom Mrs. Overdone hears, and the man of whom she tells, bad news are distinct persons. Should they be the same, however, she is not to know it until Claudio appears, for Pompey has outrun that sad little procession and enters some thirty lines ahead of it. On either supposition, the episode makes good enough stage sense.

As I read them, then, ll. 1–119 run much like this:

1–58. Amongst such dwellers in Vienna as Lucio and the 'two other gentlemen', the instant retort to danger is bravado. Rusting in peace,[1] licentious at least in speech, they boast of their familiarity with the circumstances of lechery, and its penalties.

59–82. Into the midst of their allusive ribaldry, a formidable piece of particular fact thrusts itself. Like the first clap of thunder on a sultry day comes the report, brought by Mrs. Overdone, that one of their number, Claudio, is to suffer for a breach of the neglected law, under this very head. They depart in search of more exact information; for, how should they be content, in a matter thus touching themselves, with common gossip and a general sense of its probability—that agreement with the new proclamation which they mention one to another as they withdraw?

82–119. Mrs. Overdone complains of the decay of custom—alleging many causes, but not the proclamation. There is surely no difficulty here: the only previous mention of it has not been made to her, nor (as I read it) in her hearing: it was spoken by one gentleman to his companions in the act of withdrawing, just as she was advancing to address the audience. On her servant's appearance—whether on the tail of some nameless prisoner or a little in advance of Claudio—she receives an account of the predicament of one of her customers, whose identity, clear enough at the first performance, must now be a matter of conjecture, and a warning that her business is in worse case than she has suspected: authority is putting the law in motion against her. At the first glimpse of authority's agents she is ready to move off, and Pompey stays only to inform us who it is that the Provost has in charge.

The Folio scene-division at Pompey's exit signifies no more than the departure of one set of characters and appearance on the stage

[1] A commonplace of Elizabethan social theory.

of another. Particulars of place being of small consequence on the unlocalized Elizabethan stage, we need to recognize only this: that somewhere, in this enforced passage through Vienna, Claudio encounters one or more of that little company which had set out in search of him.[1]

Juliet's presence with Claudio, when he appears escorted by the Provost and his men, and a little ahead of Lucio, is open to question. That she should be part of the unhappy train when he asks

> Why do'st thou show me thus to th' world?[2]

seems unnatural. That on both occasions when (according to the stage directions) these two are together before us,[3] they should exchange not so much as a word, surely asks some explanation. That Juliet should be present throughout a scene in which no word is addressed to her, nor does she utter any word—this is very unlikely. That she should have to hear Claudio and Lucio canvassing her share of responsibility for Claudio's predicament—this is intolerable.

If, however, Juliet is not present, then we have two references to her presence to explain away—Pompey's, and that in the stage direction; but the second may well hang on the first. Before departing, Pompey has said:

Here comes Signior *Claudio*, led by the Provost to prison: and there's Madam *Juliet*.[4]

Did Shakespeare intend to bring Juliet on, but change his mind and forget to erase the tell-tale reference? Or, did he bring her on for a brief scene of farewell, afterwards cut? If he did either, then the scribe, for his part, would be doing no more than his apparent duty in making sure that her name stood in the stage direction. Such an explanation seems more admissible than that which finds a botcher's hand to have removed Juliet's lines from the passage of dialogue between Claudio and Lucio; its texture is too close and firm.

---

[1] A producer would surely do well to accept the Cambridge editors' suggestion that the reappearance here of the two unnamed gentlemen is a mistake: the scrivener, intent on consistency, may have remembered that three had set out together and, attributing the disappearance of two to an oversight, have put them into his stage direction; but they had been merely illustrative.

[2] I. ii. 120. She may follow rather than accompany the exemplary train; but it is a cold distinction.   [3] Cf. V. i. 483.   [4] I. ii. 118.

The concluding part of this scene (ll. 120–98) serves two purposes. First, it gives us Claudio's reaction to the new situation—at Lucio's insistence. 'It is', objects Dr. Dover Wilson, 'Lucio's turn now to appear ignorant of the circumstances of Claudio's arrest, though he has been fully informed'—a too favourable reference, surely, to the tale which has provoked his impatient 'Away: Let's goe learne the truth of it'. In any case, 'to appear ignorant' is the right term for Lucio's behaviour throughout his relentless interrogation; if he were really unknowing at the outset,[1] his tone would change when he receives an answer, but there is no such change discernible.

The second purpose served by this passage is to bring within range of our imagination another character, the last to be introduced of all the persons belonging to the traditional story—and, in that story, the most important: the condemned man's sister.

Considered thus, these 198 lines of I. ii may show something of impatient and even careless workmanship, and perhaps of alterations made cursorily in compliance with some theatrical exigency; even (it may be) of change of intention in the very course of composition. What they do not (I believe) betray is such textual corruption as should forbid us to accept them as an authentic part of the play. Marks of impatience are common in the openings of Shakespeare's plays; so are traces which, like footprints already half-effaced, show recollection of his sources fading even as his own vision takes possession. Thus, the King of Hungary of whom Lucio speaks[2] as a formidable neighbour looks much like an elusive half-memory of Corvinus King of Hungary, the overlord of Julio in Whetstone's play. A man casting round absently for a name to serve some slight purpose, whether in lie or in fiction, may well find one lurking in his memory, yet never guess how it comes to be there.

The scene which follows, true to Shakespearian usage and Elizabethan stage practice, swings over to the place in which the absent Duke is to be found: somewhere outside the cognizance of the other characters—that is all we need to know of its whereabouts. It confirms an impression already faintly printed on our

---

[1] To encounter Claudio under guard is to have an unwelcome suspicion confirmed. If Lucio is shrewd enough to seek further confirmation of Mrs. Overdone's tale, he is also shrewd enough to know when he has found it.   [2] I. ii. 2.

expectation by the urgency of the opening scene. In most of the earlier versions of the story, the person who at the close redresses wrong is no more than a symbol of justice, and has hardly been heard of until he is called on to perform that function. Giraldi indeed presents him at the beginning, but is content to offer the conventional portrait of an ideal ruler, as it recurs throughout the *Hecatommithi*. Belleforest's 'Messire Charles' is likewise a pattern commander; each has delegated authority in the course of administrative routine. Here, however, is something different. This representative of supreme authority is far more prominent than his predecessors—that was to be expected, given the larger scale; but he is much less easy to understand. He is more voluble than any other character in the play, but what he utters is harder to construe, for he joins to enigmatic behaviour ambiguous comment, and mutually contradictory explanations of his purpose. Whereas the absence of the ruler in former versions had been explained in practical terms, or passed over as not worth explaining, the Duke announces that his withdrawal is of choice, and that he has reasons for it. Some of these reasons he vouchsafes to a confidant; some he promises to disclose in good time. In a closing couplet which should surely be delivered to the audience, he hints at curiosity as to the effect of power on character. His confidant, if less accommodating, might well observe that explanations so numerous are apt to jostle one another.

The identity of this confidant has given rise to doubts, of little consequence unless they breed insecurity. The list of *dramatis personae* in the Folio[1] gives:

> Thomas. ⎱ 2. Friers.
> Peter. ⎰

Thrifty persons have asked whether it was necessary that there should be two. Friar Peter, who plays an active part at the close, is mentioned by name in the dialogue.[2] This other, appearing but in one short scene, is named only in its opening stage direction. 'Peter' is so distinguished in speech-headings—necessarily, since 'Frier Lodowick'[3] is present at the same time; 'Thomas', in speech-

[1] See Appendix.   [2] IV. vi. 9.
[3] *This* name is not mentioned until necessity arises, when Isabel cites him as witness: V. i. 125.

headings, is only 'Fri.', but no further distinction is needed here. Are they really different people? I think there is some reason for believing that Shakespeare intended a difference. The Duke addresses 'Thomas' as 'holy Father', 'holy Sir', 'pious Sir', and uses him as a friend:

>None better knowes then you
>How I have ever lov'd the life removed.[1]

'Peter', on the other hand, is nothing more than an agent, to be dispatched on business without the show either of ceremony or of intimacy. If the name to which the dialogue bears no witness, Thomas, is of the scrivener's providing, his care may yet reflect stage practice: the playing of the two as distinct parts.

Accepting I. iii, then, as a scene in which the Duke discloses some part of his purpose to an interlocutor whom he holds worthy of confidence, we gain this assurance: all that he says and does relates to some design at least partly framed. As to its scope, we know enough if we recognize that it follows one of the oldest patterns of myth, folk-tale and romance, associated time out of mind with a happy ending: the story of the good prince who, unseen, will see for himself, and set all to rights.

One phase of the exposition now remains: news of Claudio's plight has yet to reach his sister. In the last scene of Act I we are confronted with the woman who has been the central figure in all considerable versions of this tale, hitherto: the counterpart of Philanira, Epitia, Cassandra. We have already learned[2] that she is a novice on the point of taking vows; that she is young, and has the gift of persuasive speech. In thus endowing her, the dramatist may have had in mind not only Epitia's rhetoric but also the demands of the situation—for, what could Cordelia or Desdemona have done in like case? In making Claudio allude to her youth he may likewise have been considering the subsequent course of the play: Isabel[3] is to prove less experienced than Epitia. But the convent

---

[1] I. iii. 7.   [2] I. ii. 182.

[3] Isabella in the list of *dramatis personae*, and in almost all stage directions; Isabel with two exceptions, throughout the dialogue: Francisca calls her Isabella; in IV. iii. 156, Lucio calls her Isabella, but presently changes to Isabel, the form used wherever she is addressed or mentioned by the Duke, Escalus, Claudio or Mariana. Compare the alternatives Juliet, Julietta—a freedom convenient in verse; also, Helen, Helena, in *All's Well*.

asks present comment. Its prominence in the design is clear. Our attention is drawn to it by the brief interchange between Isabel and Francisca: that (we may say) is how it looks from within; and by Lucio's mode of approach: he showing it from without. He is represented as having no former acquaintance with Isabel. Although, as Francisca has made us understand, she can speak with him face to face, he does not know that this novice is the very one he is seeking, but greets her as a stranger and asks her to bring him where he may find Claudio's sister. Presently, in answer to her reproof of his demeanour, he is protesting:

>   I would not, though 'tis my familiar sin,
>   With Maids to seeme the Lapwing, and to jest
>   Tongue, far from heart: play with all Virgins so:
>   I hold you as a thing en-skied, and sainted,
>   By your renouncement, an immortall spirit
>   And to be talk'd with in sincerity,
>   As with a Saint.
> Isa. You doe blaspheme the good, in mocking me.
> Luc. Doe not beleeve it: fewnes, and truth; tis thus . . .[1]

That is: to none of your profession would I use those subterfuges I practise with other women, and so let us lose no time; this is the matter. He is not, as critics seem to have assumed, offering her a personal tribute; he is marking the distance which separates the convent from the rest of Vienna—a distance clearly perceptible from either side, and kept in sight of the audience by Isabel's dress, while to their minds it is recalled by a striking reference at the climax of her appeal to Angelo.[2]

If we could come to understand this strong emphasis laid in the opening and sustained through much of the sequel on a circumstance apparently forgotten at the close,[3] we might hope at least to approach from the right direction the baffling scenes that are to follow.

The story-teller who addresses himself to children—or to men who have by no means outgrown their childish appetites—need only recount what so-and-so did. But the story-teller who hopes

---
[1] I. iv. 31.

[2] II. ii. 151. Notice, also, the terms in which other characters remark her coming and going.

[3] Isabel is, of course, free to relinquish her novitiate and marry; but her silent acquiescence in the Duke's proposal seems strange.

to hold the attention of grown men must make us understand not only what so-and-so did, but also how he came to do it—and even how it was that he *very nearly did not do it*. Indeed, it is the narrowness of the margin by which events fell out so and not otherwise that fascinates the curious imagination. And art—which can render transparent what life keeps opaque—is at liberty to show us the thing that might have been, underlying the thing that was.

Here is something more than can be conveyed by the single word 'motive'. For we have not to reckon only with the push and pull of the power that exerts itself in movement; there is, besides, that power which manifests itself in resistance to pressure—which is known through immobility. And it is the business of drama to present such forces in terms of character and circumstance, and the interaction of the two.

Of these, circumstance seems to have interested Shakespeare but fitfully: his contrivance of it is, very often, at once lavish and negligent. And, when he is in this mood, he does not build the sort of nest in which every fibre is neatly and firmly woven into its proper place, but rather the sort which (as we descry daylight through its interstices) appears almost amateurish enough for human handiwork—and yet stands up to gales from every quarter until its purpose is accomplished.

The circumstance which, at the outset, makes us understand why Isabel acted as she did, and not as Epitia and Cassandra had acted, is given in these few but emphatic references to her novitiate. Like the rook's nest, our impression of this circumstance lasts so long as it is needed. Shakespeare may himself have chosen to forget it at the close—a close, to all appearance, strangely clouded with forgetfulness.

It must be our endeavour, as we watch the play unfold, to anticipate as little as our inescapable consciousness of the sequel will allow. We may, however, occasionally pause and look round. The close of the trial of Pompey is such an occasion for considering where we stand and how we have come there. When Escalus, having disposed of Elbow and Pompey, turns to his fellow Justice—[1]

[1] Like Francisca, and perhaps Thomas, this Justice seems to serve the limited purpose for which he was called into being, and thereafter vanish, leaving no trace. This may indeed be evidence of cutting (as E. K. Chambers suggests, in his *William Shakespeare*, I. 454), but it is surely not unprecedented behaviour among Shakespearian characters.

> What's a clocke, thinke you?
> Eleven, Sir.
> I pray you home to dinner with me—[1]

we know that we are in an everyday world, however the strange, new administrative course of Angelo may impinge upon it. We know, moreover, how it compares with the worlds of the *Hecatommithi* and *Promos and Cassandra*. Penal law plays a prominent part in many of Giraldi's tales; and, while no grave charge is brought against its ministers, it cannot be said to claim our respect. In a story about a feud between two old enemies, one, having the other in his power, scorns to hand him over to the officers of the law (under which his life is forfeit), though he does not blench at the thought of putting him to death himself.[2] An image may best serve to convey the prevailing impression: the law appears as a purblind dotard, guarding an orchard; humanity, as children amongst whom it is a point of honour to rob his trees. Now and again he succeeds in catching one of these children in the act of escaping, and makes the unlucky laggard pay for all—unless a benevolent power can be invoked in time to temper his severity. This is the law of fairy-tale.

In Whetstone's play (though not in his *Heptameron*), man is presented as citizen, with some seriousness and circumstance: Whetstone, as a Tudor Englishman of ordinary capacity, being rather critical of the administration of the law than curious as to underlying principle. If Julio is indeed London, then the maintenance of justice in the London to which Shakespeare came from Warwickshire was—at least in the eyes of one zealous reformer—very faulty. A considerable share in the second part of the play[3] is given to the exposure of Promos: it is notorious that his man Phallax directs his actions, and that Phallax has his price. This, and the conduct of his officers, are brought to light by the king's councillor, Sir Ulrico, with such realism as Whetstone's poor resources allow. On the admission of the knave Rosco, all in authority have been guilty of

> Usurie, brybrie, and barrating,
> Suborning, extorcion and boulstring.[4]

---

[1] II. i. 290.
[2] The sixth tale of the first day.
[3] Much of Acts II–V.
[4] 2 *Promos and Cassandra*, II. iv.

The king sums up the case against Promos, representing what he has done to Cassandra as but the first instance to come to light of many such miscarriages of justice—

> Many waies thou hast my subjectes wrongd.[1]

To every charge, Promos pleads guilty, and, in what he believes to be his dying confession, gives an even blacker account of himself:

> Where as I lov'd, their faultes, I would not see:
> Those I did hate, tenne tymes beyond there yll
> I did persue, vyle wretch, with cruelty.[2]

And all these evil practices are illustrated in such a way as to suggest that this is the normal course of things, unless a sovereign of uncommon energy keeps narrow watch over the conduct of his subordinates. If we are to look in *Measure for Measure* for the shadows of dark thoughts on human justice, some of them will surely correspond with those in Whetstone's picture. We have been shown the two men who hold the absent Duke's commission exercising their authority in an episode which, being merely illustrative, must be supposed typical. If one of them is to play the dreadful part of the unjust judge, what should hinder the other from abetting him, if only by negligence or folly? Escalus betrays neither; and he is, to all appearance, a representative figure.[3] In a more naturalistic mode than this, it might indeed seem strange that such a man, ordained by the Duke to hold a place equivalent to that of Lord Chief Justice, should here be occupied with a case within the competence of Justice Shallow; but there is nothing in this alien to Shakespearian practice. A commonplace case is required, to illustrate the common course of things in Vienna—that variance between statute-book and public conduct which the Duke has described to Friar Thomas; and where such illustration is called for any tolerably appropriate person may be employed.

The prelude to Pompey's case is a brief but significant exchange between the two who now uphold ducal authority in Vienna. Even as they advance on to the stage, Angelo is opposing to

---

[1] 2 *Promos and Cassandra*, III. ii.
[2] Ibid., V. iv.
[3] Davenant makes Escalus into a timid old man, who would connive at anything to save his own skin.

Escalus' plea for mercy one of those oddly similar images for the law which are so diversely used by a variety of characters.—For, what reader can remember without effort which of the two similes of the despised old lion is Lucio's,[1] and which the Duke's?[2] Or, that it is Claudio who likens the neglected statutes to rusty arms hanging by,[3] and the Duke, to the rod laid aside by an indulgent father[4]—while it is Angelo who here uses the image of the too familiar scarecrow on which the birds come to perch?[5]

Escalus is intent on pleading for a milder penalty, but evidently meets with no response; indeed, this plea (like Isabel's for time) is never answered at all. He takes, therefore, a courteous liberty, asking—as an older man, a friend and one assured of the other's uprightness—'Have not even you known what it was to be rather thankful than proud of your unstained record?' And Angelo, answering (as he is often to do) not the argument itself but its upshot, rounds upon Escalus with the assertion that the law takes cognizance of nothing but the proven act[6]—concluding:

> When I, that censure him, do so offend,
> Let mine owne Judgement patterne out my death,
> And nothing come in partiall.[7]

If any doubt has until now remained among the audience, as to which of these two inherits the part of Juriste and Promos, this evident piece of dramatic irony must remove it. Angelo gives the Provost his orders for the hurrying forward of Claudio's execution —a bad course.[8] Escalus comments, in a passage of which the import is clear enough, though some of the words are certainly at fault,[9] on the inequalities of human justice; and the case of Elbow versus Pompey comes on. Angelo listens for a while impatiently, and presently withdraws, leaving Escalus to make what he can of

[1] I. iv. 64.   [2] I. iii. 22.   [3] I. ii. 171.
[4] I. iii. 23.   [5] II. i. 1.   [6] II. i. 17.

[7] Angelo's allusion, in this speech, to trial by jury seems odd; not because it is out of place in Vienna—a matter not likely to trouble Shakespeare—but because the story turns on the Deputy's sole responsibility for judgement in this very case.

[8] Lodowick Bryskett enjoins delay as safeguard of justice, recommending an interval between sentence and execution, in which the judge will consider whether the law may safely be tempered. (*Discourse of Civill Life*, p. 249.)

[9] Escalus argues that one man pays the full penalty for a single offence, while another pays nothing at all for many—so much is plain; but every line except the first seems to need mending.

the business—an Elizabethan Justice of the Peace in his own stronghold.

The writers of that age, when they discuss this office, bear vehemently either to the right hand or the left: they have neither skill nor inclination for the casting up of a profit and loss account. From them we receive either the ideal as it was framed under Henry VII and restated under his descendants; or the most extreme examples of its abuse.[1] Whetstone himself, writing in another context than that of his play, and perhaps in another mood, pays a handsome tribute to the holders of this commission:

> Mr. Lambeard and others have written learnedly and largely of the administration of this office according to Law, but much (moreover) may be said, of the administration thereof, according to Christian charitie and Justice—[2]

especially in composing differences between neighbours, patching that fabric of society which has never proved equal to the strain put upon it by human passions. Here, surely, in *Measure for Measure* is an authentic picture of that middle state between ideal and abuse. Before the Bench stand, on the one hand Elbow, with his unassailable certainty—'If these be good people in a Common-weale, . . . I know no law'[3]—and his incapacity to make it operative; on the other, Pompey; a sinner and a maker of sinners (he makes them out of such stuff as Froth), secure in the interstices of society's clumsy machinery for the maintenance of order. Escalus must do his best with what he has at his disposal, and, when this fails, rely on the authority that is in himself, the authority of experience. So —in the endeavour to ensure against recurrence of what he knows, but cannot prove, to have taken place—he aims at bringing Froth and Elbow to a sense of responsibility, one as a man of substance, the other as an officer of the crown; and Pompey to a sense of shame, or, failing this, of danger. For such a purpose, his opening modes of address are nicely differentiated: 'Friend' to Froth, 'Officer' and 'Master Constable' to Elbow; 'Mr. Tapster' to Pompey—although he knows, and Pompey knows that he knows, this appellation to be flattery. True, he is not notably successful;

---

[1] See C. A. Beard, *The Office of Justice of the Peace in England in its Origin and Development* (New York, 1904), especially pp. 134-5 (eulogy), and p. 145 (indictment).   [2] *The English Myrror*, p. 230.   [3] II. i. 41.

but the Duke himself enjoys no better success in a similar attempt;[1] nor any success at all, when he tries to bring Barnardine to a sense of what it means to own an immortal soul.

The latter part of this scene the New Cambridge editors relegate to a reviser, as unworthy of Shakespeare. But, accepting the first two-thirds, they leave Shakespeare responsible for the invention of Pompey's case, from which the colour of the scene derives. 'We stop short', Dr. Dover Wilson says, in attempting to rid the passage of un-Shakespearian matter, 'at l.187[2] in 2.1 because, to our thinking at least, there is a falling off in tone later, and because, as it happens, this point makes a convenient close to the scene';[3] and adds, in a note on l.180: 'The fun in the rest of the scene seems very tame.'

Is this curtailment so convenient? It leaves all three disputants in the air: Froth and Pompey unadmonished, and Elbow still in office. True, this latter circumstance agrees with the constable's reappearance in III. ii, and the continuance in office which that implies; but this, which could be explained on the score of administrative usage,[4] I attribute to dramatic economy.

As to the un-Shakespearian quality of this passage, I cannot discover it in the behaviour of culprits or constable, nor in Escalus' handling of them—but this must remain a matter of opinion.

As to the 'fun'—but how dispute of this at all? Johnson found 'the light or comick part' of this play 'very natural and pleasing';[5] and Johnson was not afraid to be caught looking grave when others were amused. Nevertheless, it has grieved candid readers. With those who cannot bring themselves to dwell upon it, I can sympathize—provided that they do not excuse inattention by claiming that it is aimlessly offensive. With those who, regarding it attentively, find the true strain of Shakespearian comedy here, yet wish that it had never flushed such muddy channels, I am fain to agree. And yet, if art is to preserve such components of life, let it be done by no other process than this pickling in the brine of comedy.

---

[1] III. ii. 20.   [2] l. 201 in Globe Shakespeare.
[3] New Cambridge Shakespeare, p. 111.
[4] Keeton, *Shakespeare and his Legal Problems*, p. 48.
[5] Concluding note to the play.

II. The Disputants

'Assuredly,' said Saddletree ... 'The crime is rather a favourite of the law, this species of murther being one of its ain creation.' 'Then, if the law makes murders,' said Mrs. Saddletree, 'the law should be hanged for them; or if they wad hang a lawyer instead, the country wad find nae faut.'

(Scott, *The Heart of Mid-Lothian*)

THE next phase of the play's development[1] is to be regarded as a long-drawn-out contest between Angelo and Isabel—broken *for us* by the Duke's visit to Juliet in prison, but, *for them*, despite the lapse of a night, a single, unremitting trial of strength, suspended and renewed, but never relinquished. The tension in which Angelo is held we are shown; that which holds Isabel, we are left to imagine. No character in the play serves as confidant to her: she is not shown visiting Juliet, nor returning to Francisca.

How this inheritor of the task of Epitia and Cassandra will perform it we may not guess beforehand. When Lucio had made her understand that Claudio's peril could not be averted as she first supposed,[2] she was aghast at the responsibility flung upon her, but, to his encouragement, rejoined without hesitation

Ile see what I can doe—[3]

promising to set about it forthwith, and send word of the outcome. Now, however, in her opening words to Angelo an incalculable factor is disclosed:

> There is a vice that most I doe abhorre,
> And most desire should meet the blow of Justice;
> For which I would not plead, but that I must,
> For which I must not plead, but that I am
> At warre, twixt will, and will not.[4]

Thus she stands alone, isolated from the common thought and feeling of Vienna, forbidden to use that plea which not only Lucio

---

[1] II. ii, iii and iv. [2] 'O! let him marry her.' (I. iv. 49.)
[3] I. iv. 84. [4] II. ii. 29.

and Pompey but Escalus himself has used, and the Provost recalled:
> He hath but as offended in a dreame,
> All Sects, all Ages smack of this vice, and he
> To die for 't?[1]

She may not plead, as Epitia had done and Cassandra after her, that this offence should not be judged absolutely, but in relation to the injury inflicted, the willingness and capacity to make reparation.[2] She is forbidden to use Giraldi's argument—that moral sensibility is the true instrument of judgement, discriminating amongst offences which the law confounds.[3] If we measure the distance that separates her from Epitia and Cassandra, we shall find it no less than that between Hamlet and Hieronymo. The impediment to effective action is no longer to be reckoned in practical terms, a disadvantage of situation merely; it lies in the perplexed mind and numbed will. As so often in Shakespearian practice, the reference to circumstance—here, Isabel's novitiate—has been designed to prepare us for acceptance of a factor essential to our understanding of the springs of action in a character.

It is clear that Isabel sets out with no thought of calling the law in question. Indeed, she and Angelo are at first of the same way of thinking about it, and never so far apart but that one can see the other's position. In their several situations, each has professed a stricter adherence to the principles which all Vienna acknowledges than is customary in Vienna. And, it should be observed, Vienna does not question the good faith of either. Thus, they are to dispute a matter from a shared standpoint. This is rare in art, whether of drama or novel; one reason, perhaps, why few fictitious debates stir such a tumult of response as this has done. For neither of two disputants holding opposed convictions is likely to penetrate very far into the depths of the other's, nor find the foundations of his own beliefs bared to his startled gaze. The singularity of this dispute between Angelo and Isabel may be expressed in terms of its

---

[1] II. ii. 4.

[2] For a consideration of the apparent inconsistency of Isabel's first (and only) reference to Juliet with the tenor of all she says to Angelo, see below, p. 150.

[3] The opening to this very tale, in the *Hecatommithi*, had been the wish expressed by the narrator (Fulvia) that ingratitude might be more severely punished than many acts which the law recognizes as crimes.

unlikeness to that between Portia and Shylock: neither of those two can be disconcerted by a glimpse of the other's position—still less, disquieted by discovery of his, or her, own. Their contest is as unreal as a warfare of creatures confined to separate elements. And so we never discern behind it the shadow of what might have been, lending substance to the actual event.

Isabel presents herself in some place where Angelo is accessible to suitors. That, on the unlocalized Elizabethan stage, is all that matters; and the time-honoured custom of Shakespearian editors, by which the bare scene-division, entrances and exits of the Folio are elaborated into particulars of place—'A Hall in Angelo's House', 'Another Room in the Same'—this has long been a dissipation of the reader's precious attention. Angelo is attended by the Provost; Isabel, accompanied by Lucio. The presence of both these I take to be convenient if not necessary. Both speak the common thought of Vienna on the case, but in different tones, and with difference of emphasis: Lucio, abashed in no company, can be the more voluble and explicit. That Isabel is from time to time conscious of the tone of Lucio's interjections (whether warning or encouraging her) is evident; but some may be delivered as mere conventional 'asides', like those of the Provost, while of none does she recognize the full implications.

This common opinion of Vienna Angelo is well primed to answer—so well primed that he counters it even where it has not been uttered. Herein, and in his conception of himself, lies his weakness, the weakness of assurance. It is Isabel, however, who seems to stand at a disadvantage so severe that no argument will avail—nothing but the tempests of tears and entreaties which Lucio expects, and which she does not know how to use. Since she may not condone what Claudio has done, her opening is little better than a quibble: the law, she pleads, can condemn the offence while pardoning the offender. And when Angelo retorts that the law's function would then be no more than to register a protest, her prepared position is taken, and, recognizing her case as indefensible, she makes to withdraw. But to Lucio it seems that her part is not yet begun; and, though it is unlikely that she understands what he requires of her, she returns to the attempt, with a fresh argument. Now she questions not the law but the judge's relation to it.

And who but Angelo has stirred this question? From the first, in that earlier assertion which silenced Escalus, he had identified the two: there dwelling on his own rectitude, here on his authority—

> Mine were the verie Cipher of a Function...[1]

Here is the flaw in the integrity of his thought; and always Isabel, penetrating like frost into a crack, widens it—but rather as a fugitive seeking ingress than as an assured adversary pursuing an advantage. What, she demands, is the nature of his power? 'Mortallitie and Mercie', we remember the Duke saying, 'live in thy tongue and heart'. But Angelo answers

> Looke what I will not, that I cannot doe.[2]

She presses him hard: suppose his will were towards mercy?[3] He takes refuge in the identification of himself with the officially published word:

> Hee's sentenc'd, tis too late.[4]

This does not satisfy Isabel; every human being, she persists, remains master of the word he has uttered until it has been translated into act, and, the more powerful the speaker and potent the word, the more gracious it is to take advantage of this opportunity to relent. So she is led to speak of the mercy she would show were their positions but reversed—

> I would tell what 'twere to be a Judge,
> And what a prisoner—[5]

—words as heavily charged with anticipation of a future beyond her guess as Angelo's former vaunt to Escalus—

> Let mine owne Judgement patterne out my death.[6]

Angelo, brushing aside this fanciful talk of a fantastic contingency, assures her that Claudio has in effect sentenced himself: by breaking the law he has set in motion a process which cannot be stayed. But this is to give to human law a sanction beyond what human authority can confer: the force of that Natural Law which six-

---
[1] II. ii. 39.   [2] II. ii. 52.
[3] I accept the question mark with which the Folio punctuates her sentence as signifying inquiry, and not (as often) emphasis.
[4] II. ii. 55.   [5] II. ii. 69.   [6] II. i. 30.

teenth-century jurists accepted as being ultimately of divine origin, revealed in part through the Mosaic dispensation. It is this context of thought, and the term *forfeit*, which leads Isabel, by a clear train of association, to differentiate between the burden of irredeemable debt under the old dispensation, and the promise of redemption under the new:

> Why all the soules that were, were forfeit once,
> And he that might the vantage best have tooke,
> Found out the remedie.[1]

Angelo himself is but one of those souls that must else have been forfeit. He retires behind the assurance that it is merely as an instrument of the law that he acts—and would still be obliged so to act, were his own affections in revolt against the sentence; and he attempts to bring the interview to a summary close: Claudio 'must die tomorrow'. It is not easy to guess what answer he would have found, if Isabel had pressed her objection to this precipitancy. But she is no token figure in a formal disputation; she is a living individual, with an individual's prepossessions, and the thought of Claudio's unprepared state does not primarily suggest to her the expediency of challenging her adversary on a point of law. It opens in her the vein of anarchy which runs through most of us who habitually abide by the laws, unsuspected unless authority touch some particular person. She proceeds to call the very operation of the law in question:

> Who is it that hath di'd for this offence?
> There's many have committed it.[2]

This is Angelo's opportunity. Taking her words to refer to former laxity, he retorts that severity is the truest mercy: former severity would have saved those many from offending; present severity will, though belatedly, prevent such offences from coming into existence and breeding others of the same sort. Thus, by maintaining this very rigour,

> I pittie those I doe not know[3]—

offenders that might have been. This is within the bounds of

---

[1] II. ii. 73. Given the context, there seems no warrant for Warburton's emendation (*were* to *are*).   [2] II. ii. 88.   [3] II. ii. 101.

orthodox theory, provided action be deliberate;[1] but the personal pronoun has unexpected repercussions:

> So you must be ye first that gives this sentence,
> And hee, that suffers.[2]

The particular application pleases Lucio; but his words, if they reach Isabel's ears, convey no more than general approval of the argument that is now shaping in her mind, concerning the general situation of which Angelo is no more than a particular illustration. Her thought is turned towards human authority and the power which makes it operative, and man's misconception of both: authority can only be delegated, power only lent, to the creature, but man, invested with either, supposes it his own.[3] For her, this theme of delegated authority has no peculiar aptness to Angelo's case, for it is every man's predicament. She passes on, unconscious of the effect of her words, to the inequalities of human justice in everyday transactions, the variable degree of licence permitted according to the offender's station; while Lucio, the easy-going cynic—moved by the consonance of her argument with his own estimation of persons in authority, or by what he sees in Angelo's face, or both—halloos her on; until Angelo, with defences down and face aghast, finds himself asking:

> Why doe you put these sayings upon me?[4]

She has not done so—consciously: it is the current of dramatic irony, running like an electrical charge through this passage, which makes her words dreadfully applicable, in a particular sense of which she is unaware; and she can reply without hesitation that she has addressed him simply as a personification of authority—which is what he has tacitly claimed to be, throughout their dispute—and would now ask whether the faulty stuff of human nature will stand the strain of an office which assumes perfect rectitude. She is driving home a point which Escalus, old and wise and tolerant, had kept in sheath: let him consider of what he is made, and, when called upon to judge others, recognize himself for their fellow

---

[1] See, for example, Elyot's *The Boke named the Governour* (1531), Book II, Chapter ix.   [2] II. ii. 106.
[3] For a suggested interpretation of the succession of images in lines 107, 108 and 110–23, see my note in the *Review of English Studies*, April 1951.   [4] II. ii. 133.

sinner. Angelo alone could tell how this goes home. Isabel, confident that she has found her true plea—so near, yet so distinct from the plea of all Vienna—with lightened heart offers the 'bribe' which to her has but one meaning; and, challenged,[1] proceeds, in a passage whose rhetoric is almost that of pleasantry, to assure Angelo that he need not fear from her the common implication of the term. What he does fear, has not entered her mind.

Thus, when she is hustled away by Lucio, in evident anxiety as to what she may say next, she has observed nothing which might prepare her for what is to come; but *we* have seen enough to rate at its true force the outbreak of that passion which Angelo has been smothering, and his appalled discovery of his unknown self. And so there is no need for any such clumsy device as that by which Promos discloses his own state to a confidant, and comes to terms with temptation.

Of the reality of Angelo's horror at what he finds on looking inwards, I think there can be no doubt. If we allow ourselves to be antagonized by his recollections of his own hitherto flawless integrity; by his references to himself (here, and in the soliloquy that opens II. iv) as saint and (punningly) angel; by every intimation that he holds himself apart from other men in the very act of surrender to common temptation—then we shall mistake the dramatist's intention, through disregard of his customary technique in such soliloquies.

The scene which follows,[2] between the Duke and Juliet—the only scene in which she indubitably appears—is very happily placed;[3] and yet it may be no part of the original design. It works a needed change upon the long-drawn-out dispute between Angelo and Isabel, serving a purpose not unlike that of sleep in our lives: it changes intricate preoccupation into simple sense of impending disaster. Moreover, it relieves physically, even as sleep relieves,

[1] She may be aware of Lucio's perturbation; but Angelo's exclamation would be sufficient warning.
[2] II. iii.
[3] This removal to another group of persons is a frequent Shakespearian device for marking a significant interval. If we choose to interest ourselves in circumstance, then we may say that this scene takes place on the second day of the dispute between Angelo and Isabel: the Duke tells Juliet that he is on his way to visit Claudio (II. iii. 38) and, arrived at this destination, encounters Isabel, newly come from her second interview with Angelo.

yielding a sensation as of coolness and freshness: the Duke tests Juliet, and is satisfied—here is no mere *seeming*. She expresses—for herself, and perhaps for Claudio, whose opportunities of expression are constricted[1]—acknowledgement of mutual injury and mutual forgiveness. The Duke's '*There rest*' dismisses her to a region neighbouring that in which Claudio finds himself after reconciliation with Isabel,[2] where, withdrawn from the main stream of the play, she will await recall at its close. Now, this may mean recall to our consciousness but not to our view; for the *dialogue*—the only witness we may unreservedly trust—offers no evidence of her appearance in the fifth act.

Juliet's part in the play is perplexing. The New Cambridge editors suggest[3] that it may once have been bigger: that she is, as it were, seen in process of removal. It is sometimes very difficult to be sure, in watching a figure in motion at a distance, whether it is coming or going. I incline to think that Juliet is *coming*. It may be that the dispute between Angelo and Isabel grew in the making—it impresses me as a passage which has engaged the writer even beyond his expectation; and, with such growth, the need for an interval might well become evident;[4] and to Juliet (whom, perhaps, the dramatist had not at first intended to present on the stage) may have been given the task of marking it. If this should be so, then there would emerge two possibilities, to be taken into consideration. First, in any subsequent revision, Juliet's part might well have been enlarged. (Does the indication of her presence at

[1] In talk both with Lucio and the Duke, he is preoccupied with his sentence. When the Duke assures Escalus that Claudio now accepts this sentence (III. ii. 257), we must understand that he is released from this preoccupation. The Provost's reference to 'the most gentle *Claudio*' (IV. ii. 75) indicates how he should bear himself in his later appearances.

[2] Cf. the Duke's 'Hold you there' (III. i. 175) when Claudio proposes to seek this reconciliation.

[3] 'In Juliet we seem to have a character which has got considerably out of focus through abridgment or revision' (p. 97). 'Her "part"... was probably drastically cut down in the abridgment.' (p. 130.) The part, thus reduced, could (it is suggested) have been taken by the boy who played Mariana and Francisca; but, if we have really to reckon with such stringency, surely the boy who sings to Mariana could have been pressed into service.

[4] I do not mean a mere time-interval; both Giraldi and Whetstone give this, but they occupy it with the affairs of the disputants: with an interview between brother and sister (in their two tales), disclosure of the judge's mood to a confidant (in Whetstone's play).

I. ii. 119 represent an afterthought, a notion not put into effect—at least, in the extant text?) Secondly, even if the dramatist entertained no such intention, it is possible that the players, bewildered by her sudden flowering and as sudden fading, may have attempted to remedy this apparent inconsistency in Juliet's part by insisting on her silent presence on two occasions: not only at I. ii. 119, where the dialogue invites it, but also at the discovery and forgiveness of Claudio (V. i. 494)—where there is no hint of it at all.[1]

Angelo's opening soliloquy (II. iv. 1-31) shows the advantage which temptation, like a mortal sickness, has obtained in the night. The notion that appalled him, when it first entered his consciousness, has become part of himself. The horror of it has not lessened, but his reluctance to acknowledge his new-found self encounters an equally strong certainty that to his old self there is no return. It was formerly Isabel who found herself 'at war 'twixt will and will not'. Now it is Angelo—but the will, in him, is the 'infected will' of fallen man who tastes, and loathes, and still eats, exasperated but not deterred by loathing.

Angelo's capitulation has been called in question. Objections have, in the main, followed these lines: he is a confirmed and cunning hypocrite—or else, a man of hitherto strict conduct, uncommonly ignorant of human nature, most ignorant of his own; and, in either case, conception and representation are forced and unnatural. According to Hazlitt, hypocrisy is Angelo's ruling passion.[2] But between Hazlitt and Shakespeare stood some of the greatest English novelists—and there they stand for us also; time, however, should have taught us to reckon with this impediment

---

[1] The 'improvers' of a later generation often indicate by their additions to a play their estimate of what it signally lacks. Direct representation of relationships as to which Shakespeare remains silent is officiously supplied, by Davenant in a scene between Juliet and Isabel, *The Law against Lovers*, pp. 173 . . ., by Gildon in a scene between Claudio and Juliet, *Measure for Measure, or Beauty the Best Advocate*, pp. 34 . . . . Both manifestly aim at giving Juliet a more active share.

[2] 'The only passion which influences the story is that of Angelo; and yet he seems to have a much greater passion for hypocrisy than for his mistress.' (*Characters of Shakespeare's Plays*, 1817.) Bagehot similarly argues that Angelo is a picture of a 'natural hypocrite', drawn by Shakespeare with malicious relish. (*Literary Studies*, ed. R. H. Hutton, 1879, I. 126.) Both seem to take for granted a satiric approach to the theme of hypocrisy.

in our line of vision. Now, the tradition of the English novel is predominantly comic—whether of comedy clouded by satire, or shaded by rueful self-mockery, or without any shadow at all across its smiling countenance. It is, moreover, a tradition which carries some allowance for showmanship, on the novelist's part. Thus, where his theme is the relation between *being* and *seeming*, he will present to your view now the mask and now the face, and never trouble to keep his hand out of sight. Under the influence of this tradition, we are insensibly disposed to regard the hypocrite in fiction as a man in whom the difference between goodness and a plausible imitation of it will give occasion for merriment—even, at the last, to the victims of hypocritical dealing: since the puppet-master knows, and the spectator knows, the lineaments behind the mask, and the people of the story will presently know all that is required to ensure a happy ending. (If we would test the force of this tradition, we have but to measure George Eliot's Bulstrode against any other deceiver of his fellows in the youth or prime of the English novel: to set over against our traditional showmanship that inexorable but compassionate disclosure of the naked quivering self behind the public figure; to contrast with the habitual mood of comedy that profound humour which discerns the effect of double dealing on personal relationships; to observe how far from happiness the story *must* end.) Set aside, then, this figure of the comic hypocrite which we are a little too ready to descry at the first rumour of duplicity, and who appears? Not such a deliberate impostor as Iago, who, flying the false colours of a single virtue, 'honesty', cunningly sets it off with an ostentation of gracelessness —and is by so much the more dangerous. That Angelo's reputation is no such artifact as Iago's becomes plain in his very dismay when he discovers the negligible value of all that it represents in his life. And this dismay is surely not improbable, nor is the want of self-knowledge which it betrays singular. What Angelo experiences is a discovery always in wait for the man confident of his accumulated capital of virtue. He will soon learn (like Macbeth) that to violate what he holds most sacred is to lose at once every safeguard. (Second-line troops cannot be expected to stand where the front has given way.) It is not the substance of this discovery, but what occasions it, that outgoes common experience.

Admit Angelo to be neither deceiver nor deceived in uncommon sort or measure, and the objections to this representation of his downfall must be reconsidered—as they have been, attentively, by Miss W. M. T. Dodds, for whom Angelo 'bears the marks of having been imagined intensely in all his complexity and capacity for suffering, just as Shakespeare's tragic characters are imagined, though his suffering is not fully bodied forth'.[1] This, perhaps, may be pressing a claim too far; yet I believe that Miss Dodds's plea shows the direction in which truth should be sought. I find no gross improbability here, nor any inconsistency—unless in an allusion of very slight significance: whereas the terms in which the Duke had addressed Angelo, when investing him with authority, had seemed to show him formerly a recluse,[2] the terms in which Angelo examines himself would surely hint at long continuance in public office:

> The state whereon I studied
> Is like a good thing, being often read
> Growne feard, and tedious.[3]

But this, if the first to appear, is the least of many ambiguities as to the duration of Angelo's rule, and may be considered together with others of more moment.

Isabel presents herself, and it appears that Angelo is *another and the same*: that corruption is at work in the very stuff of the man with whom we have become acquainted. Still clutching about him the rags of his public character, as though they were robes of state, he assumes an official posture, to daunt her. He knows now where she stands: he will lead her into a position from which she must plead guilty, and, involved in more insidious perplexity than the 'will and will not' of her first entry, acknowledge herself at his mercy.

Isabel seems to recognize at once that her confidence at the close of the former interview was groundless; she has not, after all, won Claudio's life, nor can hope to win it; she returns to develop a former plea, for a reprieve in which he may be prepared for

---

[1] 'The Character of Angelo in *Measure for Measure*' (*Modern Language Review*, July 1946), p. 255.　　[2] I. i. 30–41.

[3] II. iv. 7. He appears here as a man long accustomed to presentnig a composed face to the world.

death. (It is a point as to which the Duke is to be scrupulous, even in Barnardine's case.) Angelo, however, is concerned not with Isabel's cause, but with Isabel. Leaving her entreaty unanswered, he attempts to force her back into the position which had yesterday proved so advantageous to himself: doubt as to the lawfulness of her plea for pardon. He suggests that she is no better than one who pleads for the life of a murderer, and so startles her into the assertion:

> 'Tis set downe so in heaven, but not in earth.[1]

At last she shares the position of Claudio's friends throughout Vienna at large—of Escalus, the Provost, even Lucio.

It now appears why, even if Giraldi and Whetstone had not pointed the way, Shakespeare was bound to diverge from those traditional versions of the story in which the condemned man is guilty of homicide. There are not many points at which grave sin and the penal code can be directly and simply related: wrath, issuing in the act of homicide, and lust, in some of its effects,[2] make up the most part of the tale. Now, whereas it was possible for Belleforest to contrive a train of circumstances in which homicide might be extenuated, Giraldi, in which it might be pardoned even by the next of kin,[3] it could never be a matter of general and perplexed dispute, nor be characterized in the terms which all Vienna has used to Angelo, and which he has at length succeeded in making Isabel use. This, surely, explains the concentration of attention, in *Measure for Measure*, on this one sin; this, rather than the spectacular, even garish, pattern of correspondence between the fault for which Angelo pronounces sentence, and the fault for which he is eventually sentenced.

To Isabel's admission, of a rift between principle and usage, Angelo retorts exultantly:

> Say you so: then I shall poze you quickly—[4]

---

[1] II. iv. 50. It seems more probable that Isabel should intend acquiescence in the disparity between Elizabethan civil and ecclesiastical law regarding marriage, than denial of Angelo's proposition that fornication and murder are of equal sinfulness; but either way she is trapped.

[2] Puritan reformers were intent on bringing more of these within the cognizance of the law.

[3] A favourite device is to represent the man as lured or precipitated into a brawl.

[4] II. iv. 51.

and confronts her with successive hints of a hypothetical situation in which, making a choice among evil courses, she must defend the indefensible. It is as though, recognizing her intellectual integrity, he sees that she must be baffled and worsted in argument before her will can be broken. Isabel, however, supposes merely that some token of constancy is asked of her, and offers, first, to shoulder responsibility for a pardon of which the lawfulness may be in question,[1] then, to undergo any measure of bodily torment. To the ominous charge (which has rung against her name ever since)—

> Were not you then as cruell as the Sentence,
> That you have slander'd so?[2]—

she reacts, not, as Angelo had intended, in self-distrust or fear, but with simple and disinterested indignation. She finds his implied comparison between the forbearance she has invoked (divine compassion) and the leniency towards which his suggestions tend (the mutual leniency of those who connive at unlawful traffic) abominable, and says so outright:

> Ignomie in ransome, and free pardon
> Are of two houses: lawfull mercie,
> Is nothing kin to fowle redemption.[3]

It is not this he has moved for, and he brings her round sharply to face the perilous insinuation of 'slandering' the law: making light of it because (he now suggests) she thinks lightly of Claudio's offence. And this time the taunt goes home.

This is one of several passages in which Dr. Dover Wilson, finding the disputants momentarily at cross purposes, would infer textual corruption, 'There is', he says, 'no utterance of Isabella's, either in this scene or in 2.2., which would justify Angelo's accusation or her self-excuse';[4] therefore both must refer to a passage now lost. But to argue thus is, surely, to overlook the very grain of the dialogue. In a set-piece of rhetorical disputation (such as Dryden, for example, delights in), the disputants may meet one another squarely, scoring points by rule, as in a game of skill. But here is nothing of a game, of its order and limitation. The two

---

[1] An offer which reverberates in the close of the play, when she undertakes a like responsibility in pleading for Angelo.
[2] II. iv. 109.   [3] II. iv. 111.   [4] New Cambridge Shakespeare, p. 134.

have been locked in a conflict as engrossing and desperate as though they wrestled on the edge of a cliff, the loser to go over. And each, so extended, has made strange discoveries, Angelo about himself, Isabel about the cause she is pleading. For him, this has been a dreadful experience, and he wishes her to undergo its equivalent and be forced to acknowledge some inner rottenness; while she has learnt to plead human frailty, and at length to frame her plea in terms that would have startled her self of yesterday; and, in the impetuosity of her pleading, she has used unflattering language of human justice and its agents. I will go so far as to say that, whereas a lesser craftsman would have maintained logical equipoise, this very departure from logic seems to me an excellent reason for accepting the whole as Shakespeare's handiwork, neither rationalized nor sophisticated by any other hand.

Isabel is now indeed perplexed; Angelo has out-manœuvred her. The argument from human frailty, on which she had yesterday counted to extricate Claudio, is turned against her: she is reminded of all she has urged as to the flawed fabric of human nature. What business has such a being with scruples? She is presented with the monstrous terms of ransom, and left to discover where she stands.

I have traced the course of this dispute minutely, with a particular object in view: to show it as a clash alike of ideas, and persons; to obtain recognition of the equal importance of character, and function, in the disputants.

To the passage which follows, the seventeen lines with which Isabel concludes the scene, we must make a fresh approach, not prejudging its significance as a measure of character. It has given very general offence, and (though some of the objections raised betray negligent or wilful reading) a persistent distress of this kind is not to be lightly argued away: words and phrases are not repeatedly mis-read without some prompting of inclination or repulsion, and where such prompting is general it demands explanation. Isabel's lines, here, must be considered in the large context of Shakespeare's habitual treatment of his women. To none[1] of them does he assign a soliloquy, properly so called: no passage,

[1] Helena's opening of her heart to herself (*All's Well that Ends Well*, I. i. 90) may perhaps rank as an exception.

that is, of thinking aloud and following, willy-nilly, where thought leads. Apostrophes are given them, rhetorical or poetical—Constance's or Juliet's; confidences shared with the audience, most often delicately comic, whether the tone be sprightly or rueful, Rosalind's or Viola's; confidences spoken in the presence of servants, though directed askance—Portia's, while she waits for news from the Capitol; explanations, some delivered with an outspoken plainness which has disconcerted their admirers.[1] But they do not walk with themselves and talk with themselves, as his men are sometimes permitted, sometimes compelled, to do. Such a passage of self-exploration as Angelo's, in the close of II. ii, never awaits Isabel; she is never to waylay herself. To this general rule, even Lady Macbeth's sleep-walking scene is no true exception; it is by phantoms that *she* is ambushed. Lady Macbeth, reading her husband's letter; Juliet, waking by her husband's body; Imogen, by the body she supposes her husband's; all these may be said to *address* someone, even though he must be invoked from the dead, or from absence: they are not forced upon their own society. In sum, the women of Shakespeare's plays are unacquainted with the impulse to introspection, incurious about themselves. Not, I believe, because he was incurious about them, or curious to no avail: the dramatist who could be present in imagination with Hermione among her women could have followed her into solitude; nor, because he grudged them range of ideas or command of language: Hermione again, Imogen—even Cordelia, supposedly taciturn—would disprove that. It is because of the peculiar function he assigns them that they are rarely if ever explorers of their own minds. If we discriminate broadly, we shall not find among their ranks a tragic character—unless it were Isabel; notably, none that are tragic as Phaedra is tragic. Many of them are sufferers by tragic calamity; often, they are themselves the occasion of tragedy, by reason of this very inability or disinclination for introspection: an unconcern, or incapacity, to understand what they themselves are, or what they seem to others; to guess what construction may be put upon their words or actions. That is, of

---

[1] Raleigh was troubled by the employment of Shakespeare's 'most cherished characters' in 'the menial explanatory work of a chorus', and instanced Cordelia. (*Shakespeare*, p. 170.)

course, one explanation of the favour with which they have been always and everywhere received; set aside the few who are downright bad, and we may say of any or all what Isabel says of Mariana: 'I have heard of the Lady, and good words went with her name.'[1] Simplicity can harbour no conflicting thoughts: no tragic decision is theirs to take, nor conflict to resolve. The possibility of regarding Isabel as an exception to this rule can be assessed only when her share in the whole play is within view. Meanwhile, it has to be admitted that here is another, and not the last, of those difficult transitions on which the charge of inconsistency brought against this character is grounded.

For the present, it must be enough to recognize that these seventeen lines[2] serve a purpose: they crystallize the situation (even for the slower witted in that mixed audience with which an Elizabethan playwright had to reckon).[3] It is worth while to compare them with a passage in *Romeo and Juliet*. As in Juliet's speech, when she comes to a recognition of her own situation,[4] the first few lines are flung after the retreating figure of a newly discovered adversary ('Ancient damnation...'—'O perilous mouthes...'); the remainder addressed to the audience, in direct explanation of the approach intended towards another from whom compensating support is expected ('I'll to the friar...'—'Ile to my brother...')—in this instance, a disastrous approach, for it assumes an obligation lying with equal weight upon both, acknowledged on behalf of both with a large impersonal certitude. 'Had he twentie heads... hee'ld yeeld them up...' 'More then our Brother, is our Chastitie.' This is not the taking of a decision, but the proclamation of a foregone conclusion.[5]

There remains, now, a single phase of this struggle: Isabel's passage with Claudio, the only part of the play comparable, for intensity, with the passages between Isabel and Angelo—at least until the end is within sight. It does not form a separate scene, but so sharp is the sense of interruption and change of tension where it begins and ends that those parts of the scene which precede and

---

[1] III. i. 219.   [2] II. iv. 171-87.
[3] This surely holds good in some degree even of the audience at a court performance. It must be remembered that any audience of that day would include some whose modern counterparts seek their pleasure elsewhere than in the theatre.
[4] III. v. 235.   [5] For a consideration of ll. 184, 185 of this scene, see Appendix.

follow it appear but as prologue and epilogue. Thus, the prologue would consist of the discourse delivered by the Duke, in his assumed character of friar, to the condemned man—Claudio's silence heightening the sense of expectancy.

The Duke's admonition has troubled some whose very prejudices are worth hearing. It has been censured as bad divinity: Claudio is invited to regard life as an unwanted gift, of which a well-judging man will gladly disembarrass himself—and may do so, for good and all, by death. This accords strangely with the religious habit which the Duke has put on. It shocked Johnson; but there were elements in the context with which he may not have reckoned. We have only lately learned how curious an amalgam of moral precepts drawn from ancient philosophy, the Bible and the writings of the fathers, would be set before a thinking, reading boy, in an Elizabethan grammar school;[1] and been shown what vein of mediaeval thought runs through Elizabethan tragedy.[2] A difficulty nevertheless remains: death as the culmination in this world of the consequences of Adam's transgression had been recommended as a wholesome subject of meditation, but not without complementary ideas of another world; and of this other world the greatest Elizabethan tragedy has little to say. It is in the absence of any such reference that Johnson descries the shadow of pagan thought falling across the Duke's homily:

> I cannot without indignation find Shakespeare saying, that *death is only sleep*, lengthening out his exhortation by a sentence which in the *Friar* is impious, in the reasoner is foolish, and in the poet trite and vulgar.[3]

The sixteenth-century moralists, however, were sometimes content to accept from ancient philosophy precepts pointing *towards* conduct in keeping with Christian doctrine; whether these pointed anywhere else, beyond or beside the approved aim, they seem not to have asked.[4]

[1] T. W. Baldwin's *William Shakspere's Small Latine and Lesse Greeke* (University of Illinois Press, 1944). See especially Chapter xlviii.
[2] Willard Farnham, *The Medieval Heritage of Elizabethan Tragedy* (Berkeley, 1936). See especially the Conclusion.   [3] Note on III. i. (III. i. 17.)
[4] For a succinct account of the vein of Lucretian thought in the Duke's homily, see L. C. Martin, 'Shakespeare, Lucretius and the Commonplaces' (*Review of English Studies*, July 1945).

In another sort of context, that of the play, this passage is certainly apposite; and yet a doubt attends this very aptness. The Duke warns Claudio against setting an inordinate value on life; in terms which would not disconcert that first audience, he invites him to ask himself: 'At what rate should I buy such a commodity?' The question is very much to the purpose—supposing only that the speaker knows Isabel to be coming, and on what errand she comes. But how should the Duke know that Claudio is to be given the opportunity of buying his life, at a price?

This is only the first of several occasions on which we are teased by the question: What does the Duke know? Something may be gained by framing it, even from the outset, in general terms. In any relation of incident, part of the pattern must be formed by the juxtaposition of those who know, and those who do not know. One among the people of the story knows, another thinks he knows, and yet another is all too well aware that he does not know, whose name is written in the will, who was admitted on such a night—or, whatever may be in doubt. And, where interest is confined to intrigue, all these particular circumstances must be exactly defined; for intrigue is nothing if not smart, nor is smartness attainable without neatness. But there is another sort of knowledge attributable to characters in fiction: posed by the entire story, disclosed at least in part during its course, reverberating beyond its limits. Of such knowledge, and such characters, we do not ask: With what particular facts is he at this moment acquainted?—any more than we should inquire how many, and which, of the circumstances of Ophelia's death were made known to Hamlet, and when, and where; since it may be said, in brief, that we are concerned to know what Hamlet learns about death, rather than what he learns about the death of Ophelia. Thus the problem resolves itself to this single, simple but not simply answered, question: What sort of character is the Duke? And this, like the problem of Isabel's consistency, must await further evidence.

Hard upon the Duke's assault follows Isabel's. It contrasts sharply with the tenderness and magnanimity of Epitia's bearing when she yields to Vico's entreaties—even, with Cassandra's less gracefully expressed compliance—and it has been censured accordingly. Reacting against the vehemence of such censure, R. W. Chambers argued that Isabel takes the best possible way with Claudio[1]—but to me this appears only the generous extravagance of one who means to be satisfied. Charlotte Lennox, an intrepid woman, quite without critical sense or the self-distrust it breeds, offered to point out the way that Isabel should have taken[2]—and so many readers have shared her dissatisfaction that some must surely have envied her courage. In reconsidering the grounds of this dissatisfaction, it is necessary to remember that the persons of a drama have before them the choice of ways allowed them by the dramatist, neither less nor more. Thus, Cordelia has a choice between the way that Goneril and Regan have already taken and the way she eventually takes; and Isabel may fairly be said to have a choice between the way formerly taken by Epitia and Cassandra, and the way she is now to take. That discreet, tactful middle way which we can all point out to fictitious characters in such a predicament is neither here nor there; it may exist in life, but is not to be reckoned with in art unless the artist has himself chosen to offer it to his creature. It has, moreover, no place in criticism unless the artist has failed to obtain our acceptance of his framing of the dilemma, for the people he has made, in the predicament he has devised.

In the passage of explanation with which she concluded her last conflict with Angelo, Isabel has clearly conveyed to us her sense of the situation: in hearing her story, Claudio is to receive the assurance that he is 'yielding up his head' not merely because punishment is to be inflicted on him, but because it is his part gallantly to sustain a refusal of dishonourable terms. But to Claudio her intimation is less explicit—it is indeed wrapped and muffled in fold upon fold of strange imagery. And he, in the agony of bewildered suspense, must reiterate his question: to what conditions does she darkly allude?—until at last he startles her into acknowledged doubt of his steadfastness with the intensity of his demand:

Let me know the point—[3]

that is: 'Give me the facts, and let me decide for myself this ques-

---

[1] *The Jacobean Shakespeare and 'Measure for Measure'*, pp. 41, 42.
[2] *Shakespear Illustrated*, I. 33. [3] III. i. 73.

tion of values at which you repeatedly hint.' Obtaining from him, in answer to her high-pitched protest, brave assurance, she plunges again into the tale that she can never quite bring herself to tell, but still, possessed with the recollection of her encounter with Angelo, looks back rather than forward, and treats the issue always as a foregone conclusion. To what she is able to disclose, Claudio seems[1] to listen in shocked incredulity. But the resolution that accompanies it is no more than momentary. It is followed by a succession of increasingly abstracted murmurs of assent to her inopportune commendation and consolation. Both disputants move as we seem to move in a nightmare, refusing to acknowledge what is upon us. Suddenly, and incoherently, the question breaks from Claudio: 'Can the transaction really be unpardonable, since it is the wise Angelo who proposes it?'—as unhappy an approach to Isabel in her anguish, as hers, to him. And now the issue is open at last between them: it is life itself that she has been keeping hidden in her figurative, allusive talk—his life, which she could give him, and will not. And, though the Duke's arguments may have stripped life of splendour, nevertheless it now appears to Claudio as the alternative to a mode of being wholly intolerable—body and soul alike suffering torments of every sort that human fear has taught men to expect.[2] Hence the terror which finds utterance in his entreaty, and the answering terror which impels her reply: an exchange which is the more shocking because we see her in a position to translate into action the cruel words that fear prompts. For though her denial is grounded in principle, the expression of it is framed by passion—the disfiguring passion of fear.

Johnson wrote of the murder of Desdemona: 'I am glad that I have ended my revisal of this dreadful scene. It is not to be endured.'[3] As much might be said of this passage—more, indeed, if the dramatist has failed to obtain our acquiescence in his design: if

[1] His first reaction is obscured by what I take to be a ghost-word—'prenzie' (l. 94); which recurs, as a slip is apt to do, at l. 97.
[2] L. C. Martin suggests that Claudio (in ll. 118-28) 'reflects, with some exactness, the mental state of the man who, according to Lucretius, has failed to banish care because he cannot use himself to the thought of complete extinction'. ('Shakespeare, Lucretius and the Commonplaces' (*Review of English Studies*, July 1945, p. 180)). The passage has also been canvassed by E. M. Pope and T. W. Baldwin (*Shakespeare Quarterly*, July and October 1950). For a further suggestion, see Appendix. [3] Note on *Othello*, V. vi. (V. ii. 83.)

we may still object to his limitation of the courses open to his characters as arbitrary, or protest with Charlotte Lennox that we can see nothing to prevent them taking another way. It may be significant that Charlotte Lennox herself has no sooner opened this *third door* than she finds herself in quite another play: one in which Isabel, after reasoning with her brother, is to yield to his entreaties. In her estimation (that is) an Isabel who was in a condition to argue the case would not be able to sustain her refusal. (There is very often a core of common sense in this lady's independent opinions.) To canvas the *might have beens* of those who have indeed no being, the persons of a story—this is rash at best, and, at worst, futile. But thus far I wil lventure: if the play had followed the course which Charlotte Lennox recommends to the conclusion of the matter as it now stands—if Isabel had remained both collected and resolute—we should find it unendurable. This does not, however, exhaust the possibilities. Suppose argument to be out of the question—what should hinder Isabel from the use of that 'prone and speechlesse dialect' which Claudio reckoned her most precious talisman?[1] That there is a hindrance in which drama's reliance upon speech is but one component, I am convinced. Comparison with another treatment of this theme may serve to show the conflict between Isabel and Claudio as one in which neither—given what the dramatist gives, the characters, the situation, the train of events, and given no more and no less—could have acted differently.

The predicament of these two seems to have haunted Walter Scott. In *The Heart of Mid-Lothian*[2] we may discern a parallel deliberately traced alongside *Measure for Measure*, with chapter-headings for sign-posts. As the crisis draws near, in which Jeanie must commit perjury or withhold from her sister the hope of acquittal, a number of these chapter-headings are taken from appropriate passages in the play;[3] while verbal echoes are heard in the narration—George Staunton, for example, writing to Baillie

[1] I. ii. 188.

[2] The following passage was written some years before Dr. Tillyard published his comment on the parallel between play and novel, in *Shakespeare's Problem Plays* (1950). I have allowed it to stand unaltered.

[3] Vol. II, Chapters vi, viii, x, xiii, in Edinburgh edition of 1818, from which I quote throughout.

Middleburgh of 'a law so cruel, that it has hung by the wall, like unscoured armour, for twenty years'.[1] Scott has, indeed, been at pains to emphasize the likeness of situation: the law by which Effie must die—and which is obnoxious to the good people of Edinburgh as well as to the rogues—is the outcome of former laxity and precipitate legislation. There is some adjustment of balance: thus, Effie is not a sympathetic character, but the scales are weighted in her favour—it is entirely clear that she has not killed her child. There is, moreover, insistence on her youth, as there had been on Vico's; whereas Isabel, to judge from Claudio's first mention of her, would seem to be the younger of these two. Her plea is therefore doubly strengthened, and the word which Jeanie cannot speak on her behalf may fairly be represented as substantially true, since it will lead to a true verdict; and Effie may regard Jeanie's scruple as of no moral consequence—of force only for a conscience which to her appears excessively tender and exact. She extracts from her sister the admission that her life hangs on this thread, and thence proceeds relentlessly:

'And he wanted you to say something to yon folks, that wad save my young life?'

'He wanted,' answered Jeanie, 'that I suld be mansworn.'

'And you tauld him,' said Effie, 'that ye wadna hear o' coming between me and the death that I am to die, and me no aughteen year auld yet?'

'I told him,' replied Jeanie, who now trembled at the turn which her sister's reflections seemed about to take, 'that I dared na swear to an untruth.'

'And what d'ye ca' an untruth?' said Effie . . .

Presently:

'O, if it stude wi' me to save ye wi' risk of *my* life!' said Jeanie.

'Ay, lass,' said her sister, 'that's lightly said, but no sae lightly credited, frae ane that winna ware a word for me . . .'[2]

Thus, with a clarity which the relationship between women makes possible, the stubborn point at issue is exposed: the one who must deny a plea for life would willingly give life itself, but cannot forsake principle; the one who pleads has at heart no such regard for that principle as would stand in the way if the other's life were in

[1] Vol. II, p. 138.   [2] Vol. II, pp. 206-8.

danger.[1] Moreover, Jeanie knows or thinks she knows that everyone whose opinion she values expects her to surrender this principle for her sister's sake—the passage at cross purposes with her father seeming to range him with the rest; and she has time to weigh this expectation and all it implies against her own conviction. How is it, then, that little of the censure which falls on Isabel has touched her?

One, perhaps the most cogent, reason for this amnesty is her steadfast gentleness in her dealings with her sister; and I think it is sometimes forgotten that this is the gentleness which strength can give. Jeanie knows herself the protector; Isabel looks to Claudio for protection and, finding none, reacts with a violence resembling the motions of one who has clutched at a support only to find it come away in his hand. Another reason for the differing response to these two characters lies outside literature, and yet it ought to be mentioned: when Juliet exclaims against the law which grants her life and takes that of her lover;[2] when Isabel protests that she would gladly give her life to save her brother's;[3] they wake disquieting reverberations in a world where it is tacitly assumed that, in the ordinary course of things, violent death always stands nearer to any man than any woman.[4] Thus, Jeanie's 'O, if it stude wi' me to save ye wi' risk of *my* life' and Effie's unfair but unanswerable retort—'Ay, lass, that's lightly said'—stir in the reader an even more painful response when the issue lies between a man and a woman.

Yet another reason for the contrasted reactions to Isabel and Jeanie may spring from the deep-lying differences between Elizabethan drama and nineteenth-century novel. Scott, working within that convention which allows the novelist to establish tacit understanding with his readers, turns it to account for conveying to us the relation between Jeanie's integrity and her simplicity. Now, simplicity in a character not predominantly comic,[5] and in respect of grave concerns, is delicate stuff to handle. It cannot be

---

[1] Cf. *Measure for Measure*, III. i. 104–6.   [2] II. iii. 40.   [3] III. i. 184.
[4] This disquiet sharpens perceptibly in time of war.
[5]   Love, therefore, and tongue-tied simplicity
         In least speak most, to my capacity (M.N.D., V. i. 104).
So Theseus says, and the sequel justifies his confidence. But this simplicity is comic, and the occasion merry.

presented, as it were, in a vacuum—unsupported—save where it speaks to us in suffering rather than in action; or, where it is the stamp of a minor character (most often, very young or very old); or, where it is associated with one of transient importance, endowed with speech but for a significant moment—a Juliet or a Mariana. Jeanie's simplicity is not left unsupported. In the long, still reaches of the novel, and in his own ample, unhurried manner, Scott establishes complementary qualities, and devises a variety of occasions for eliciting them. He presents in several aspects a woman who is inarticulate about the things that lie near her heart, voluble about the concerns of her capable, busy hands, and—this is a subtler touch—ready enough to answer on a point of conscience where the form rather than the substance of her faith is called in question. The lawyer in Scott gave the disputation between Jeanie and the elder Staunton; the sympathetic observer of common life gave that talk of practical affairs which overflows when once anxiety is eased; the poet in him gave the language of her appeal to the Queen; but it was the story-teller's art which designed all these to complement her broken phrases and silences, when entreated by Effie and George Staunton. The contrast is broadened eventually to farce, for Scott's fine sense of direction did not always tell him where to stop; but even at its broadest it never violates the integrity of the character, and the amplitude which allows it is a necessary condition of that character's life.

Scott's advantage is not, however, to be reckoned only in terms of space and leisure. There is something else to be taken into account, and it is of his own making. When he cites the Covenanting conscience to explain Jeanie's scruples, he is not merely presenting her to an easy-going England, or a Scotland seemingly forgetful of past rigours and splendours; he is presuming on a warrant, for which he has himself obtained unquestionable validity, to transmit matters whose authenticity has been established by history or tradition. His sense of the past—which is a sense of modes of thought and feeling common to a whole people in some former age—and his incomparable power of communicating this sense—which has altered the cast of our imagination—enable him to set certain springs of action, in his characters, beyond cavil and even beyond question.

Thus, an Elizabethan dramatist (no matter how strong) may leave us in doubt where the inheritor of Scott's estate (however weak) can be explicit; although, since this literary kind of inheritance is not the whole tale, it is still possible that a great historical novelist—even Scott himself—might give a clearer account of Jeanie's scruples than of Isabel's. There is a singular rigidity in her bearing, not to be altogether explained by her separateness from the rest of Vienna; but whether it conveys the dramatist's sense of a character under strain, or betrays the strain under which he sustains that character, we shall not be in a position to determine until the end is reached.

Angelo's case also requires suspended judgement. He seems to derive something from Juriste: inexperience, with a dangerous excitement in the exercise of power; something perhaps from Lupton's judge, who is well aware of his own shining reputation.[1] He has nothing in common with the mere scoundrels of Belleforest and Goulart; nothing, so far, to suggest Promos and those characters of the older allegorical drama into whom evil enters and from whom it withdraws at the instigation of agents who are rather personifications than persons.

Of the lesser characters, those that have so far appeared have declared themselves. About Escalus, we probably shall not learn, nor need to learn, much more. Of Claudio we are to see very little more: the Provost's references[2] seem to imply that, like Juliet, he now awaits the final pardon in a sort of retirement from the main current of the play.[3]

---

[1] N. i. r.   [2] E.g., IV. ii. 64 and 75.
[3] Of the little he has to say, in this retirement, nothing is prosaic; his report of Barnardine is disturbingly poetic, alike in imagery and cadence. This may account for the deep impression he left on Pater.

III. The Arbiter

'Nec deus intersit nisi vindice nodus inciderit.'
                              (Horace, *De Arte Poetica*)

THE part of the play which now follows, extending to the eve of the trial, leaves a very different impression from the great scenes of dispute, and asks a different handling, in the analysis.[1] It is as though a stream which has hitherto made its own channel were here forced to seek outlet, seemingly in vain; but it should not be forgotten that the impetus formerly felt may now be accumulating, ready for the instant when an outlet is found.

The text of this part of the play is in many passages open to suspicion, and in some certainly at fault. I believe, nevertheless, that the faulty pieces may be distinguished and isolated: that they need not spread the contagion of doubt through the rest. They can be so isolated, however, only if problems which show some likeness one with another yield to explanations similarly related. It will not be enough, for example, to explain away discordant time-references severally, nor to account one by one for the succession of enigmas with which the Duke in his progress seems to confront us.

The dominant question to be considered is this: does the whole, or a substantial part, of this stretch of the play make *stage sense*? Does it yield a practicable and (once the proper mode of presentation is ascertained) intelligible stage performance? I have already[2] offered an opinion as to the way in which we should treat Folio stage directions and act- and scene-divisions. What libery of interpretation will be ours when we come to the very fabric of the text —dialogue, which (we may hope) is at worst a faulty transcript of what Shakespeare wrote? This: we may fairly recognize that— even at the best—it conveyed something less than his whole intention: that he was in a position to fill in the interstices that any dialogue must leave gaping with instructions delivered by word of

---

[1] Pater interprets this impression in terms of 'flagging skill', a descent into 'homely comedy' and loss of the 'grander manner' of the earlier part of the play. (*Appreciations*, p. 178.)   [2] See pp. 44–6, above.

mouth and enforced with all the authority of his position in the theatre. We are therefore at liberty to consider, with due caution, any presentation which the dialogue does not forbid, nor even discourage, and which, for its part, lends coherence to the dialogue.

Thus, I must ask leave to play the producer for a while, in that ideal theatre—built as near as may be to the Elizabethan plan—which every careful reader must keep in being, within his imagination. I have suggested that Act III should be regarded as a single, unbroken passage, as it stands in the Folio; and I believe that we shall, by so regarding it, discern in its development rather fluidity than inconsequence. Let me, therefore, begin with its opening, and allow it to play itself out in my theatre of the imagination, claiming no more liberty than is required for frequent amplification, and occasional reconsideration, of stage directions. I assume the use of inner and outer stage, and, if necessary, of the balcony also. If place indications help the reader, let the inner stage stand for a cell, affording some sort of privacy; the outer, for any other place within the confines of the prison; the balcony, for one affording some concealment, from the view of those on the stage. This, then, is what I would have the audience see.

The Duke and Claudio appear upon the inner stage, already deep in their subject: the Provost need not appear (despite the entry which the Folio gives him in the scene-heading) until Isabel's voice without (at l. 44) summons him to activity.[1] Upon her entry, they two exchange a word on the outer stage, she mentioning her business, he giving her welcome—the Duke and Claudio meanwhile engaged in parting courtesies on the inner stage. Isabel joins Claudio here while the Duke, drawing the Provost forward, requests that he may remain, unseen by them, and withdraws to some coign of vantage. It is not necessary that this should be within our field of vision—we have been admitted to the secret of his presence; but it may be convenient to keep us aware of it, for thus his separation from the Provost will be marked; the Provost, whose ignorance of what is spoken on this occasion forms part of the design,[2] must now be supposed to remove beyond hearing. On

[1] If he is present during these first 44 lines, then it is as an official and onlooker merely.
[2] The Duke assumes it when, in talk with the Provost, he refers to Angelo's

the inner stage, Isabel and Claudio engage, until the Duke's intervention releases them. By a few words he ensures *her* stay (she remaining, ungracious but acquiescent, on this inner stage) and, drawing *him* forward, tells him—first, that he has been eavesdropping (a tale he will relinquish on turning to Isabel), then, that Angelo was but proving her—and this is a story which *she* must on no account overhear, for she would contradict it outright; besides, all her subsequent intercourse with the Duke shows her ignorant of it. He now wishes Claudio away; releasing him, therefore, to join his sister on the inner stage, he summons the Provost with raised voice (thus marking the independent entry of one whom he would not acknowledge for a collaborator in his design), and dispatches them together.[1] He thus secures the whole of Isabel's attention, and the opportunity to open a subject of which none but she must hear. He proceeds with her in good order: first, a sententious but brief address, by which he recommends himself to her in his assumed character of spiritual counsellor; then, a rapid, succinct development of his proposal. Isabel at first mistakes his drift, supposing that the question—what she will do, to 'content' Angelo—is but *his* terms of ransom over again; and, steadfast in her denial,[2] looks only for retribution. This gives him an opening for his first point: not even from 'the good Duke' can she hope for

integrity (IV. ii. 82), and presently undertakes to prove that it has failed here (IV. ii. 166). No more is required to prepare us for this than that the Duke should appear alone on the balcony.

[1] It will be seen that I have modified the Folio stage directions only by giving the Provost an entrance. I have departed from the stage directions of modern editions in these particulars: I have deferred Claudio's departure for six lines; for, while Isabel remains on the stage, the conjunction of 'Let me ask my sister pardon' with *exit* makes poor sense; and I have delayed the Provost's entry until he is addressed by name (that is, by half a line), and presently dispatched him and his charge together. This gives opportunity for a brief dumb-show of reconciliation between brother and sister. Two objects are gained by these minor re-arrangements. First, the Duke's peremptory summons and dismissal of the Provost now makes sense: his 'Leave me a while with the Maid' means: 'Leave me alone with her; take him away.' Secondly, the loose end of Claudio's 'Let me ask my sister pardon' becomes a connecting thread; and it is not sentiment alone that demands some show of reconciliation. True, the time afforded for exchanging forgiveness is very short; but, where words are unavailing, brevity is best: they are not to measure out mutual contrition.

[2] If this seems to conflict with the suggestion of a show of reconciliation, it should be remembered that they are reconciled on these terms, tacitly.

redress, since she lacks a witness. This is a factor in the situation which is to be kept constantly before us;[1] the Duke presents but one aspect of it to Isabel when he tells her that Angelo will claim to have 'made trial of her only'. His own credence, he has already hinted, rests on some secret, and supposedly unchallengeable, source of information: 'Fortune hath convaid to my understanding . . .' He now completes the capture of her attention by suggesting that an effectual design exists, in his own brain, and proceeds to unfold it with notable economy of language. In the seventy lines before her dismissal, Isabel is informed of the past and present relations between Angelo and Mariana, given sufficient opportunity to express recollection, assent and eventual reliance on the narrator, and acquainted with a project—of which just so many details are suggested as will convince the audience that they carry in their heads the whole of an intricate design. This is not slack writing. The prose, though it carries little stamp of individuality, is workmanlike. True, it relaxes the emotional tension; but that is required to mark the transition to a new phase of the play, and so we may not infer that the tautness of the dramatist's own mind was relaxed.

In sum, I believe that all these 281 lines[2] make good *stage sense*—not merely the first 150 of them; and that we should be chary of rejecting any passage for which so much as this can be claimed.

Hard upon Isabel's departure, on her mission of feigned compliance, follow three successive episodes, adroitly connected. The outer stage may now suggest to our imagination the common court of the prison, to which prisoners are brought on their way to closer confinement. As in IV. iii, it is—by day—easy of access to all comers: Isabel and Lucio make their way in and out with small ceremony.

Having dispatched Isabel upon her errand to Angelo, the Duke, I take it, remains[3]—drawing a little apart until he is observed and

---

[1] Cf. the Duke to Lucio (III. ii. 176), and the whole treatment of the problem of evidence in the trial scene.

[2] I.e., the first 281 lines of Act III in the Folio; in modern editions, III. i.

[3] It is true that he has promised to go forthwith to St. Luke's; true also that his arrival there (IV. i.) will seem belated. The dramatist, however, requires his presence *here*—and has not yet, I dare say, faced all of the problems involved in this intricate passage of intrigue, nor devised means for dealing with such of them as might perplex the audience.

hailed by Elbow. To him enter various persons, succeeding one another in groups or singly: first, Elbow and subordinates,[1] with Pompey in charge. Pompey, intractable to Escalus' warning, is not likely to heed the Duke's: his confidence is in his own powers of ingratiation and the accommodating texture of society which has hitherto afforded him shelter. This confidence is first called in question by the next comer, Lucio, on whose particular countenance he had reckoned; and Lucio's rebuff is the opening of a passage charged with ironic implications. Taking the Duke at a disadvantage, imprisoned within his assumed character, he makes the most of his opportunity[2] and leaves his victim to reflect on calumny, until the entrance, severally,[3] of Escalus, the Provost and Mrs. Overdone. The Duke has now to contemplate further evidence of Angelo's activity in stirring the muddy channels of his city; and this leads naturally enough, as the lesser persons withdraw,[4] to a passage of general reflection addressed to the audience. Since this passage—twenty-two lines in a measure for which the rest of the play affords no counterpart—has been called in question even by conservative critics, I should like to set it aside, as questionable, until I have analysed those successive episodes which divide it from the Duke's intervention between Isabel and Claudio.

Notice, first of all, that one person alone remains present[5]

---

[1] Here, as in Claudio's progress to prison (I. ii. 120), the Folio gives 'Officers'.

[2] It is, of course, the dramatist who is conscious of the opportunity, not Lucio; but the audience will not notice this.

[3] The Folio's 'Enter Escalus, Provost, and Bawd' would, if taken at the foot of the letter, give an inappropriate escort for Mrs. Overdone. Modern editors assign her to the care of such 'officers' as lately brought on Pompey. I suggest that this is what we should see on the stage: Escalus, whose business is with the Provost, enters as the 'officers' are handing over to their superior their bedraggled charge; her struggles and clamour attract Escalus' attention, and he pauses to admonish her and to comment on her case—and on that evidence from Lucio which has brought it to official notice—before opening the matter about which he has come to inform the Provost: the failure of yet another appeal on Claudio's behalf. His reference to preparation for death gives the Provost opportunity to draw forward the supposed Friar; the dramatist, to clear the character of the 'absent' duke.

[4] Since the Provost must outstay Mrs. Overdone, to effect a connection between Escalus and the supposed Friar, and since there is no occasion for a separate exit, he may stand aside through the 50 lines of their conversation together, coming forward at its conclusion to conduct Escalus towards the inner prison.

[5] My removal of the modern scene division between Isabel's departure and Elbow's entry with Pompey has merely emphasized this, not brought it about.

throughout these comings and goings, and that this one is so situated that he can, and does, address the audience directly when any transaction among the others requires comment. The Duke here occupies such a position as Shakespeare occasionally assigns to one of his characters: a position which he has not formerly held, but which he assumed, directly and unmistakably, upon his entry to Isabel and Claudio (III. i. 151). At that instant when he intervened between them, the play's centre of gravity was palpably shifted: the burden was transferred—a transference marked by the simultaneous change from verse to prose.[1] When the Duke tells Claudio that Angelo has never meant to corrupt Isabel—'onely he hath made an assay of her vertue, to practise his judgement with the disposition of natures'; and when he goes on to exhort him: 'Do not satisfie your resolution with hopes that are fallible, to morrow you must die',[2] he is saying something which, if spoken by an actual person, could not be called anything but a lie; but, spoken by a fictitious person of a particular sort, may fairly bear another title. He deliberately *misinforms* his hearer inside the play, presenting him with information which on his own reckoning is false[3]— for he has no doubt whatever as to Angelo's purpose,[4] and every intention of preventing it. Nevertheless, he is *informing* us, his hearers outside the play—presenting us with information which, on his own computation, should eventually prove true; for his words carry an intimation of what he means to fashion out of the situation—even, in some sort, what he has already made of it. In his design (as it is here foreshadowed and beginning to assume substance) this is how those characters who have hitherto carried the play's burden are now situated: whereas Angelo has insisted, Isabel has tacitly admitted, and Claudio has believed that it is in her hand that his life lies, to give or to withhold, it now becomes plain that his hope of escaping death must lie elsewhere. Nothing remains for Isabel to keep or to surrender; no decision now rests with her— that burden has been lifted from her. In the place once occupied by

---

[1] This change has nothing in common with the unaccountable verse-prose alternation of IV. i.   [2] III. i. 162 and 170.
[3] Even the falsehood might be defended as salutary; it was hope which had undone Claudio.
[4] Not only what he says to Isabel, but also his whole course of action makes this clear.

an impulsively compassionate gaoler now stands a figure for which former versions offer no precedent; one in whose hands the Provost himself will be an agent merely. Isabel will, it is true, still have a part to play; but so will every other character—except Juliet in her retirement, and the clowns (Pompey, Elbow, Abhorson) in their comic unconsciousness of the very element in which they have their being. All the rest will be cast for one part or another in the Duke's moral interlude.

That he should stand fast, while others come and go, now begins to appear significant. He may be likened to the producer of a play whose humour it is that the players should know no more than their own parts—and who must therefore stand by to direct any concerted action; or the strategist who must be at hand to control developments—for, since the stuff in which he is working is (supposedly) life itself, he may find himself fast in the very web he is weaving. This at least is certain: he, remaining immobile, should engage our steady attention; it is his reaction to these comers and goers that must make their significance plain to us. Pompey and Mrs. Overdone—separated by their client, Lucio, and so deployed as to appear representative—impress upon the Duke the security of that traffic which the exercise of constituted authority in Vienna has failed to put down. Lucio's contribution to this impression, although it may appear as simple as theirs, is indeed composite. On the surface it expresses the sort of comic insight which informs popular proverbs, shrewd and often spiteful: eavesdroppers hear no good of themselves; one who has placed himself in the Duke's predicament must continue to listen, whether he will or no, and is likely to learn that he is generally reckoned ineffectual abroad and, if all were known, no better than he should be at home.

A little below this, another vein of comedy appears, still broad: the tables turned yet again. Lucio, having extracted from Pompey the admission that he is on his way to prison, exclaims exultantly: 'Why 'tis not amisse *Pompey*: farewell: goe say I sent thee thether.'[1] In such rigmarole as his, no unsupported assertion need signify much; but this one does not stand alone. Presently Mrs. Overdone is to mention him in terms which bear out its implications. Appealing against her own arrest, she says: 'This is one

---

[1] III. ii. 65.

Lucio's information against me.'[1] In the interim, Lucio has been offering information against the absent Duke—not, it is true, in a quarter where reward will be forthcoming, but he heightens his charges and piles up circumstance like one rehearsing a tale of which he means to make use. Now, it is part of Whetstone's satiric purpose to show informers multiplying under Promos' rule: in one of the loosely illustrative episodes that he uses for representing the state of Julio, a clownish fellow is blackmailed by Phallax and his bullies, who persuade him that he has incurred the severity of the new law by kissing the maidservant in his father's house.[2] Rigour has bred dishonesty, encouraging clever rogues to fish in troubled waters, and simpletons to buy them off rather than face authority. Lupton sees the matter differently: in Mauqsun, every citizen is a potential informer, and proud of it; and Whetstone's pamphlets suggest that he himself came to regard this practice as a city's only safeguard.[3] But Shakespeare's audience is not likely to have been of this opinion, and with every proffer of information by Lucio, here and at the final trial, their pleasurable expectation of his discomfiture must surely have been heightened.

The Duke's final interrogation of Escalus serves more than one purpose: lest Lucio's words should have bred doubt, it reassures us as to the estimation in which his reputable subjects hold the Duke, and it sustains *his* quest of that elusive distinction between being and seeming, of the line that separates what a man is, and what his fellows suppose him. It sustains also our interest in this quest, and in its outcome.

It is surely becoming evident that the knowledge which the Duke is now engaged in pursuing is of a different sort from that which may be measured in terms of its value to the intrigue. (Thus, we are probably little the poorer for want of answers to such questions as the story itself prompts: How soon was he acquainted with Angelo's questionable treatment of Mariana? And, with what particulars was he primed when he visited Claudio in prison?) This knowledge, then, is something other than information; and yet I believe that we should not call it experience: it has not enough in common with the knowledge to which Shake-

---

[1] III. ii. 210.   [2] 2 *Promos and Cassandra*, III. ii.
[3] *A Mirour for Magestrates of Cyties* (1584).

speare's tragic heroes win, by doing and suffering, for the Duke himself does not engage our concern by what he does, or suffers. How, we may fairly ask, does he—or should he—engage it? Criticism has for some while inclined towards the opinion that here is one of those persons in Shakespearian drama who should be regarded as important in respect rather of function than of character, and are to be interpreted as we should interpret the principal persons in allegory.[1] Now, the language of allegory is at least approximately translatable. These persons, therefore, must stand for something that can be expressed in other than allegorical terms, and the concept for which the Duke stands be capable of formulation in such terms as criticism may employ. What is this concept?

This is not an easy question to answer, nor are the answers so far proposed easy to discuss. Since those that suggest a religious allegory, and hint at a divine analogy, are shocking to me, and cannot be anything of the sort to those who have framed them, it must follow that my objections are all too likely to shock in their turn. This offence is apt to be mutual; for, where reverence is concerned, there is even less hope of reaching agreement by argument than in matters of taste. I would not willingly offend; but there is not room for compromise.

Let me recall the burden of the popular tale of the monstrous ransom: the situation in which the woman, the judge and the ruler confronted one another signified power, exerted to its full capacity against weakness, and weakness (reduced to uttermost misery) gathering itself up to appeal beyond power to authority. Expressed thus, in simple and general terms, it seems indeed analogous with that allegory of divine might invoked to redress abuse of human inequality which is shadowed in Browning's *Instans Tyrannus*. But it should be remembered that such simplification obliterates one particular which, if fairly reckoned with, might forbid religious analogy: in the old tale, the ruler was distant, ignorant, brought to intervene only by uncommon exertion on the part of those whom his absence had exposed to oppression;[2] and none of the amplifications designed to make the tale more

[1] This opinion is shared by those who find in the play an explicitly Christian meaning. See p. 41, above.
[2] For this absence, a reason is usually given—seemingly, to forestall censure.

H

acceptable had done anything to shift or reduce this untoward circumstance. Indeed, by magnifying the whole, they made the part more obvious.

Lupton's *Siuqila* beyond the rest develops that element in the story which draws us to think about the maintenance of justice, not merely in the version it gives of this tale but also in the similar tales surrounding it.[1] And it is notable that, whereas this one tale is told by the wretched Siuqila to show that even in his own country one who has no longer anything to lose will tell all and thus bring about retribution, Omen's tales are told to illustrate the happier state of Mauqsun. The theme of three of them is the success of the good ruler who goes about his domain *incognito* to discover and redress wrong. In one, a judge who waylays and interrogates suitors is able to rescue a woman from oppression.[2] In both of the others, the king himself is shown using disguise and similar subterfuge, not only to obtain truth but also to make it publicly apparent. In one,[3] he learns by means of his 'privie Espials', who ride about the country at his command in the character of private gentlemen, the plight of a woman who has been ill used by her stepson. He hides her at court and lets it be rumoured that she is dead; and, after much handling of witnesses, confronts the offender with his victim, and delivers sentence. The other tells how he 'changed his apparell, making himselfe like a Servingmã, and went out at a privie Posterngate, and so enquired in the prisons, what prisoners were there', and was able to confute the cunning oppressor by bringing him face to face with the oppressed.[4]

Now, in all these variations on a single theme, the activity of some magistrate or ruler—going about or sending out his agents, in disguise—*assists* in bringing smothered truth to light. Reflecting on opportune intervention in one,[5] Siuqila sums up the moral of all: 'It was only the Lords working, that putte it into his heart' to speak with the woman who was secretly oppressed, and into hers to tell this stranger what she has hitherto forborne to utter; for 'God works al this by marvellous means, if we would consider it, for the helping of the innocent and godly'.[6] Even under an ideal

---

[1] See p. 23, above.
[2] T. iii. v. to X. i. r.
[3] R. ii. v. to T. ii. r.
[4] Y. iii. v. to Z. ii. r.
[5] The story of the ill-used stepmother.
[6] R. iv. v.

system of justice, that is, the discovery of wrong might well be impossible were it not for the intervention of divine providence, which, on some particular occasion, puts it into the heart of this or that human agent to make a pertinent inquiry. Now, this is in keeping with popular thought, which comes very near to supposing an element of caprice in divine government,[1] because it does not look ahead, but complacently descries pieces of pattern in particular events, without considering the ugly unreason of the total design which such parts must compose. But, how fearfully the distance between this false start and its logical conclusion diminishes, if the ruler is regarded not as agent but as emblem of divine providence! It is difficult to believe that those who would have us interpret the Duke's part so can have followed the implied train of thought all the way.

The centre of gravity for this interpretation is the passage in which Angelo capitulates to the alliance of knowledge and power in the reinstated Duke:

> Oh, my dread Lord,
> I should be guiltier then my guiltinesse,
> To thinke I can be undiscerneable,
> When I perceive your grace, like powre divine,
> Hath look'd upon my passes.[2]

On this Professor Wilson Knight comments:

> Like Prospero, the Duke tends to assume proportions evidently divine. Once he is actually compared to the Supreme Power.[3]

So to argue is surely to misunderstand the nature and usage of imagery—which does not liken a thing to itself. Yet this argument has been widely accepted; if not unreservedly, yet with reservations which do not reach the real difficulty. To suggest that the comparison may have been made 'unconsciously' by Shakespeare, and to admit that 'both the Duke in *Measure for Measure*, and Prospero, are endowed with characteristics which make it impossible for us to regard them as direct representatives of the Deity, such as we find in the miracle plays ... Prospero, at least, [having]

---

[1] This is well exemplified by the speech of Whetstone's compassionate gaoler, after he has released Andrugio (1 *Promos and Cassandra*, IV. v.).
[2] V. i. 371. [3] *The Wheel of Fire* (1949), p. 79.

human imperfections'[1]—this is not enough. There will, of course, be human imperfections in any human representation, most plentiful where least desired, for what we ourselves are is most evident when we declare what we would be, in the endeavour to represent ideal beings. But observe where the prime fault occurs, in the character of this ruler: he is to blame in respect of the performance of that very function in virtue of which he is supposedly to be identified with Divine Providence. Read the sentence

> ... I perceive your grace, like powre divine,
> Hath look'd upon my passes

as the figurative expression which its syntax proclaims it—that is, as a comparison proposed between distinct, even diverse, subjects in respect of a particular point of resemblance—and it yields nothing at odds with the accepted idea of a ruler who, despite the utmost exertion of human good will, must still be indebted to a power beyond his own for any success in performance of that duty which is entailed on him as God's vice-regent, and who, when such success visits his endeavours, will transiently exemplify the significance of that vice-regency. But, exact from that same sentence more than figurative expression has to give, and you are confronted with the notion of a divine being who arrives (like a comic policeman) at the scene of the disaster by an outside chance, and only just in time.

Treat the whole story as fairy-tale, and you are not obliged to challenge any of its suppositions. Treat it as moral apologue, expressed in terms proper to its age, and it will answer such challenge as may fairly be offered. The Duke's expedients will then serve to illustrate the energy and resources of a human agent. But, suppose him other than human,[2] and the way leads inescapably to that conclusion which Sir Edmund Chambers reaches, when he

---

[1] S. L. Bethell, *Shakespeare and the Popular Dramatic Tradition* (1944), pp. 106–7. See also Leavis, 'The Greatness of *Measure for Measure*', and Traversi, '*Measure for Measure*' (*Scrutiny*, January and Summer 1942). V. K. Whitaker ('Philosophy and Romance in Shakespeare's "Problem" Comedies' in *The Seventeenth Century* by R. F. Jones and Others, Stanford U.P., 1951, p. 353) suggests that this passage approaches as nearly to a reference to God 'as Shakespeare could come under the law of 1605 against stage profanity'—an explanation which raises many more questions than it answers.

[2] For the extreme form of this supposition, see Battenhouse, '*Measure for Measure* and Christian Doctrine of the Atonement' (*Publications of the Modern Language Association of America*, December 1946).

reflects on this play: 'Surely the treatment of Providence is ironical.'[1] Unless *Measure for Measure* is to be accepted, and dismissed, as simple fairy-tale—and what fairy-tale ever troubled so the imagination?—the clue to this central and enigmatic figure must be sought in representations of the good ruler as subjects of a Tudor sovereign conceived him; above all, in those illustrative anecdotes which writers (popular and learned alike) were glad to employ, and content to draw from common sources.

A number of these are to be found associated with the name and reputation of the Emperor Alexander Severus.[2] Developing on a course similar to that taken by Guevara's Marcus Aurelius romance, this curious legend was for a spell popular in England. Its fullest, most circumstantial and most influential exemplar I take to be Sir Thomas Elyot's *Image of Governance*.[3] Here the salient features of the ideal portrait are these: inheriting a legacy of disorder and corruption, the good emperor is zealous in the reform of manners by means of social legislation and the careful appointment and assiduous supervision of his ministers of justice. To ensure a just outcome he will intervene in a case by subterfuge, not merely employing spies but acting in that capacity himself, and, when he has detected wrong-doing, not content merely to bring the accused to trial, he will handle the witnesses, cause false information to be put about, and trick the culprit into pronouncing his own sentence.[4] One after another, Tudor and Stuart sovereigns were addressed obliquely through anecdotes of Alexander Severus, congratulated on resemblance to him in respect of those virtues which the writer most desired in a ruler, and delicately invited to put to opportune employment those powers and qualities of which the country stood in need.[5] These pseudo-historical anec-

---

[1] *Shakespeare: a Survey* (1925), p. 215.

[2] For an account of this legend, its development in England and range of application, see my article: 'Sir Thomas Elyot and the Legend of Alexander Severus' (*Review of English Studies*, October 1951).

[3] *The Image of Governance Compiled of the Actes and Sentences notable, of the moste noble Emperour Alexander Severus* (1541). This purports to be a translation from a Greek work by the Emperor's secretary, supplemented from other sources.

[4] See particularly Chapters viii to xix, xxiv, xxxviii and xxxix.

[5] For an illustration of the adaptability of Elyot's anecdotes, see Whetstone's *Mirour for Magestrates of Cyties*, apparently a free version of those that Whetstone found congenial to his own times, and temper.

dotes, of which more than one bears a resemblance to those in Lupton's *Siuqila*, are many of them commonplaces of popular fiction; but, used by writers whose main intention was not to tell a story (either historical or fictitious), they illustrate an idea of the business of government which could then be seriously canvassed by men involved in that very business, or eager to advise those so involved. They chart the tides and currents that a writer for an Elizabethan audience must have reckoned with, and remind us how far the direction of these habitual sympathies and antipathies has since altered: thus removing some of the obstacles to a fair estimate of the Duke's conduct.

Another part of time's obstruction may be loosened by a close comparison at particular points of *Measure for Measure* with Middleton's *Phoenix*. This again is a disguise-story. Now, the man present in disguise is the man left out of the reckoning by everyone else. The situation his presence creates is charged with that sort of irony which the stage can use to fullest effect. Moreover, the difference between what he knows and may communicate to us, and what the rest of the people in the play suppose, can be broad comedy for the simpler part of the audience, yet take on a finer edge for quick and reflective minds.

When Phoenix proposes to find out the true state of affairs under his father's rule, he obtains leave to depart without ceremony, attended only by a chosen friend:

> For that's the benefit a private gentleman
> Enjoys beyond our state, when he notes all,
> Himself un-noted.

Evil can evade a prince's scrutiny:

> ... if I appear a sun,
> They'll run into the shade with their ill deeds,
> And so prevent me.[1]

Alone with the companion of his travels, Fidelio, he explains that he holds it best,

> ... since my father is near his setting, and I upon the eastern hill to take my rise, to look into the heart and bowels of this dukedom, and, in disguise, mark all abuses ready for reformation or punishment.[2]

[1] I. i. 59 and 66. [2] I. i. 99.

There is thus both likeness and difference between these two, the man left out of the reckoning in either play. They are alike in what they undertake. But, whereas the Duke accepts responsibility for the suspected evil both seek to uncover, Phoenix can attribute it to his father's enfeebled state and injudicious lenity. This certainly smooths the way to the happy ending; but it may perhaps explain why the acquisition of wisdom on which his father congratulates him when he finally abdicates in his favour has to be taken on trust. His sententious observations in the course of his discoveries have marked no advance on his original confidences to Fidelio. What he has acquired is in fact merely information—worth not a farthing beyond its value to the intrigue.

It is in this context, of traditional and popular stories which essay (with more or less seriousness) *of government the properties to unfold*, that we have to understand the eleven couplets which the Duke delivers to the audience at the close of Act III: before that scene at the moated grange, which alone relieves the succession of prison episodes stretching from the failure of Isabel's appeal to the eve of the trial. The substance of these lines is appropriate to the speaker and the occasion: the first four are general and sententious, advancing a proposition which is upheld elsewhere in the play[1]— that personal rectitude is the most important qualification for a magistrate; the next two bring this generalization to bear on Angelo; of the remaining five, the first two are obscure, but— taken in conjunction with those that follow—suggest that ill designs may be thwarted by corresponding 'craft' directed to good ends; the last three particularize—the Duke intends to turn the tables on Angelo, using the means which he has already mentioned to Isabel.

The form, however, of these twenty-two lines is obviously questionable. They have been called octosyllabics, which is surely misleading, and likened to the Gower choruses in *Pericles*, from which they differ signally. Those, while they sustain their initial impulse,[2] are a spirited imitation of fourteenth-century octosyllabic verse—as it were, a Rowley-poem before its time; these go to

---

[1] E.g., at IV. ii. 82. Here, admittedly, the *application* is ironical, but there is no reason for supposing the proposition so.

[2] They presently subside into lame decasyllabics.

another tune. The staple is a line of seven syllables, which proceeds with a rocking motion from a strong beat in the opening to a strong beat in the close—'Patterne in himselfe to know'.[1] It is capable of easy expansion, in any of three ways: by a light syllable at the end, giving a disyllabic rhyme ('More, nor lesse to others paying'); by a light syllable at the beginning, giving a regular octosyllabic line ('To weede my vice, and let his grow'); by a heavy syllable at the beginning, leading to a ripple of light syllables before the rhythm re-establishes itself ('Craft against vice, I must applie').

Now, the closest metrical counterpart to these couplets, within the compass of Shakespeare's plays, is the epilogue to *The Tempest*, spoken by Prospero;[2] and the only place where verse of this sort would be proper is prologue or epilogue—or, where its substance forbids either supposition, as it does here, a formal pause midway. For a play in ten acts, such as Whetstone's, it would indeed be necessary, as prologue to the second part; we cannot, however, suppose it a survival from a lost play closely modelled on Whetstone's, because it requires an active ruler, a feigned submission by the woman, and another end than his in view. One conjecture remains permissible; at some performance,[3] Shakespeare's play was given in two parts, a pause intervening, and on this occasion it was judged prudent to remind[4] the audience, on renewal of the performance, of the theme and situation. For such a pause, this, the resolution of a train of episodes in which the Duke has had opportunity to assess his undertaking, would be appropriate enough.

Act IV opens with a song which may or may not be Shakespeare's. The evidence, though often canvassed, remains insufficient, the argument inconclusive. The single stanza which the boy sings to Mariana may have been written by Shakespeare, or provided by a maker of songs for this play on the occasion of some

---

[1] It is possible that more lines were once of this sort, e.g.:
      Who the sword of heaven would bear
      Should be holy as severe.

[2] Though this has no light ending nor disyllabic rhyme, it contains the other three types of line, and fluctuates easily between seven and eight syllables.

[3] Probably, part of some festival, at court or great house; perhaps, on the original occasion, the Christmas revels of 1604.

[4] Remind, not inform; the manner is allusive.

performance; or it may be one of two stanzas written—whether by the dramatist or another—for Fletcher's *Bloody Brother*.[1] On the first supposition, Fletcher—or someone concerned about his play —took the single stanza and added to it one of his own. On the second, someone, at some time before the issue of the First Folio, took from Fletcher's manuscript that part of the song which could be sung on a woman's behalf. Even though the song were to be certainly ascribed to another than Shakespeare, we should still be at a loss to know whether it replaced one of his or was inserted where none had been.[2] Where the area of doubt is so overgrown, speculation is futile. All that can usefully be said is this: of the possibilities with which we have to reckon, more than one implies some disturbance of the text. If a song has been added, so likewise have the accompanying references to it; if it replaces one lost, that loss may not be limited to the song.

The text of this scene is indeed questionable on many counts. Mariana's opening contains a curious time-reference:

> Here comes a man of comfort, whose advice
> Hath often still'd my brawling discontent.[3]

This would suggest that Angelo's rule had already lasted some while; whereas the impression hitherto conveyed has been one of precipitancy—events following in quick succession on his assumption of power. The passage between the Duke's entry and his first words to Isabel is awkward in several respects. The change from verse to prose seems pointless and flat, the intrigue thick and muddy. Obtaining an assurance that he is the first comer (though he had told Isabel that he would be there before her[4]), he forgoes his advantage, and, hustling Mariana out of the way, gets from Isabel that very information which must be communicated to Mariana—who is only then recalled to hear it, in dumb show. Six lines' length is all the time allowed for accompaniment to this latter transaction; and in these six lines the Duke harks back incon-

---

[1] First printed 1639, but, according to J. D. Jump, 'Written—in part, at least— either during or before 1625'. (See his edition, 1948.)
[2] We do not know nearly enough of the provision of songs in Elizabethan plays. Cf. the problem posed by those in the folio of Lyly's.   [3] IV. i. 8.
[4] He had promised to prepare Mariana (III. i. 268 and III. i. 278), and enjoined Isabel to 'call upon him' at the moated grange (III. i. 278).

sequently to his former theme of calumny. I cannot believe that we have here what the dramatist intended. Johnson's comment on the conference between the women sets the problem in daylight, but it does not solve it. 'There was', he says, 'a necessity to fill up the time in which the ladies converse apart, and they must have quick tongues and ready apprehensions, if they understood each other while this speech was uttered.'[1] Such colloquies, that is, and the indifferent dialogue which marks their duration, obey the laws not of probability, but of dramatic convention.[2] True, but it is not a dramatic convention that the persons concerned should have been playing hide-and-seek under our eyes immediately beforehand.

Now, if the part of this scene which runs from the Duke's greeting to Isabel as far as his dismissal of the two women upon their business is examined separately, it is seen to differ from its context by reason of its tough coherence. With the exception of a single rent—and that not past mending[3]—it is in strongly woven verse, and the argument, designed to inform us of the mechanism of that intrigue which the Duke has already projected,[4] is well knit. If we take the song and its immediate context for after-thought or intrusion (a working hypothesis), we obtain an opening to the scene much like this: the Duke, meeting Isabel at Mariana's door, greets her and inquires how she has sped in her errand to Angelo; she recalls one by one the injunctions which must be observed by the woman who keeps Angelo's appointment, and he—either telling her how he has 'framed'[5] Mariana, or explaining why he has not done so—knocks at the door. When it opens and Mariana admits the two, we may take it (if we wish to be particular) that they three now stand within Mariana's house. On this supposition, we have another disturbance of the text to reckon with at the end of this scene: to correspond with the former, it should involve the loss, either of some reference by the Duke to past converse with Mariana on his proposal, or of present opportunity for such an exchange—which, we cannot guess. One emendation, however,

[1] Note on IV. iii. (IV. i. 60).
[2] Notice that the colloquy between Brutus and Cassius (II. i. 100-11) is of another sort: they are concluding an argument of which we have heard the beginning, and have been invited to guess the middle.
[3] See Appendix.   [4] III. i. 255-72.   [5] That is, briefed.

may fairly be attempted here: to move the Duke's six lines ('Oh Place, and greatnes . . . in their fancies') to another position, adjacent to his other four lines on calumny ('No might, nor greatnesse . . . slanderous tong').[1] This was Warburton's proposal, but he did not suggest any arrangement of the composite passage, and modern editors[2] have preferred to set 'Oh Place, and greatnes . . .' after 'No might, nor greatnesse . . .', whereas the alternative order has something to recommend it: if the six lines should precede the four, they would together compose such a passage as may, within the convention of the formal soliloquy, be delivered to the audience; apostrophe, the release of pent-up bitterness, is calmed to sententious observation, and *sentence* clinched with a couplet.[3]

How these disturbances could have come about, and their outcome be the Folio text, is another question, my every conjecture depending upon a tissue of supposition whose fabric has still to be examined, and, so far as possible, tested, when the end of Act IV is reached.

The part of the play which now lies immediately ahead poses its own problems, but they are (I believe) of a different sort from those belonging to IV. i, not involving the supposition of interference, merely that of indecision on the dramatist's own part, or decision not completely implemented; in which case it should be possible to trace the course of his unfolding design through the successive episodes which compose IV. ii and iii.

The initial fooling of Pompey with the Provost should confirm, in minds familiar with the usages of Shakespearian comedy, the surmise that no one is going to die. In Shakespearian tragedy, the clown may caper round the doomed characters, may even be a minor agent of catastrophe, as in *Antony and Cleopatra*; but the irony with which his presence charges the situation is bound up with his unconsciousness of its tragic implications: mortality is his theme, but dying and putting to death were never further from his thoughts. When Pompey, on the other hand, or Posthumus'

---

[1] IV. i. 60 . . ., and III. ii. 196. . . .   [2] E.g., New Cambridge Shakespeare.
[3] All ten lines suit the instant of Lucio's departure much better than the midst of Mariana's business; that is, the move must take this direction. The difficulty remaining in my arrangement, the incomplete line 'And racke thee in their fancies', may result from the attempt to join the shifted passage of soliloquy to the passage of dialogue which now concludes the scene.

gaoler, fingers penny cord or axe, and indulges in such grim pleasantries as the taste of the age encouraged, we know that the hangman's rope is tow, the headsman's axe, lath. Three words only are designed to make any sharp and particular impression: those in which the Provost couples Claudio's name with that of one, Barnardine.

This opening gives place to an exchange between Pompey and Abhorson which is manifestly incomplete: a riddle is posed but not answered; an allusion glances back to a proposition which has not been uttered. Between lines 50 and 51 a brief passage is surely missing; not necessarily lost, for the whole has the appearance of a first draft, in which what is required may be inserted presently. The quibbling over, Pompey—his old ingratiating, canine self—takes service with his new master, and both are dispatched to summon Claudio and Barnardine, that the two condemned men may hear each the time fixed for his own execution.[1] Left alone for the space of two lines, the Provost makes the only mention which the play contains of the offence with which Barnardine is charged:

> Th'one has my pitie; not a jot the other,
> Being a Murtherer, though he were my brother.[2]

The couplet is flat and harsh; but it is the content, rather than the form, that sets all the bells jangling: from this point onwards, Barnardine is associated with unquiet overtones and discords never resolved.

Before I begin to trace this curious development, let me indicate one problem which is (in my judgement) resolved by Barnardine's course through the play. If the author of *Measure for Measure* should ever come to learn of the theory that he designed to recommend himself to the new sovereign by presenting his duke as a flattering emblem of royal wisdom and benignity, he would need to call but one witness—Barnardine. It is neither here nor there that Lucio attempts to bring the Duke's name in disrepute, and achieves something—we are to understand that every public name is at the mercy of idle calumny—nor, that he is punished for it. So likewise Proditor speaks ill of Phoenix and the old Duke his

[1] The time-references respecting the execution present a difficulty of no great consequence. See Appendix.   [2] IV. ii. 64.

father, and is punished. These reversals, comic or ironic, are proper to the intrigue; they are not felt beyond it. But the repercussions of what Barnardine does to the Duke are felt, not merely throughout the rest of the play, but beyond. For, while Lucio impinges on the Duke by what he says, Barnardine's impact is charged with the peculiar shock of what he is. Barnardine is the old soldier by the Scottish cross-roads; he is the poacher in the shadow of an English spinney; the man who will always, without effort or apparent intention, make constituted authority appear ridiculous—especially in the person of his interlocutor. Escalus and Elbow would have fared alike with him. To express a sense of the ludicrous change that independence works in the aspect of authority is by no means to call authority in question; but to represent that incongruity in a conversation-piece, juxtaposing a Barnardine, or an Edie Ochiltree, with authority personified—this is to produce a picture in which one would not wish a royal patron to discover his own likeness. Judged as flattery, such a representation could only be ironical—or uncommonly off-hand. Favourable acceptance might be hoped from a man very dense, very vain, reared in the softest circumstances: without these three to blunt discernment, the charm will never work. The newly come king was not such a man. As to the dramatist, his well-wishers at court had never reason to say of him:

> I love not to see wretchedness o'ercharged
> And duty in his service perishing.

It is surely time that we heard the last of that supposed connection between the Duke's sagacity, and *Basilikon Doron*;[1] and with it the notion of a dramatist deeply disquieted by the corrupting influence of power, yet intent on flattering, in the person of his patron, the highest representative of that power.

It is time to trace Barnardine's short, erratic but ineffaceable course. When Claudio enters, in response to the Provost's summons,[2] the names of the two men have been coupled and Barnardine's associated with a crime which sets him in antithesis to Claudio: condemned, not by Angelo but by common opinion.

---

[1] See L. Albrecht, *Neue Untersuchungen zu Shakespeares Mass für Mass*. I find nothing in James I's political writings to support the view that Shakespeare intended any echo of the king's opinions to be recognized in this play. [2] IV. ii. 65.

Claudio's first reference to him, and the Provost's rejoinder, develop the contrast in a way which becomes fully intelligible only when Angelo's letter is under discussion between the Provost and the Duke.[1] His name having here been joined, yet again, with Claudio's, the Duke (whom Angelo's precipitancy has compelled to review his own plan) seizes upon it and asks: 'What is that *Barnardine*, who is to be executed in th' afternoone?' Having learnt something of the case (though nothing of the crime), he continues, in his assumed character: 'Hath he borne himselfe penitently in prison? How seemes he to be touch'd?'—and gets this answer: 'A man that apprehends death no more dreadfully, but as a drunken sleepe, carelesse, wreaklesse, and fearlesse of what's past, present, or to come: insensible of mortality, and desperately mortall.'[2] Except for an echo, which I must suppose unintended and unlucky, of the Duke's recent attempt to persuade Claudio that sleep and death are one, this passage seems to complete deliberately the impression we are to receive of Barnardine as Claudio's opposite: where Claudio thinks with too vivid and particular imagination on what it will be like to be dead, Barnardine is incapable of imagining that state at all. 'Conscience' makes a coward of Claudio; the want of it makes Barnardine a brute. Thus, I find so far no hint of after-thought or improvisation, no perfunctory provision of a nonentity demanded by the exigencies of a recalcitrant intrigue, but rather the fashioning of a character who, even before his first appearance, is recognized as integral to the play's design. It is indeed when Barnardine appears that the perplexity about him begins.

The Duke has obtained that ascendancy over the Provost which the plot now requires, first by the proffer of *stage proofs*, then by the spell of poetry. On the withdrawal of these two figures, the prison wakens: the former night-references[3] give place to those of dawn.[4] Pompey presents himself in a passage of commonplace fooling with which any clown might be furnished by any drama-

---

[1] IV. ii. 123.   [2] IV. ii. 149.
[3] 'Tis now dead midnight ... (IV. ii. 67). The best, and wholsomst spirits of the night ... (IV. ii. 76). As neere the dawning ... as it is ... (IV. ii. 97). Notice also the Provost's consternation at every knock, and the business of 'calling up' the officer, to open the gate.
[4] Looke, th' unfolding Starre calles up the Shepheard (IV. ii. 219).

tist, or might even furnish himself. Presently Abhorson joins him, and they bend their attention to the business of Barnardine; so, indeed, does everyone in the prison—to little apparent effect. If Barnardine was really created for no other purpose than to do Claudio *a present and a dangerous courtesy*, it is surely odd that the whole resources of authority in the prison should be engaged in obtaining his compliance; odder still that it should prove unobtainable, and that a character called into being only to die, should survive. The situation captured Hazlitt's imagination.[1] It prompted Raleigh to tease dull readers with the pleasant suggestion that 'Barnardine, a mere detail of the machinery, comes alive, and so endears himself to his maker, that his execution is felt to be impossible. Even the murderer of Antigonus has not the heart to put Barnardine to death.'[2]

Now, this is *very gracious fooling*; but it fails, or perhaps refuses, to take into account one fact. Whetstone's compassionate gaoler had explained, after dismissing Andrugio to refuge:

> ... See how God hath wrought for his safety?
> A dead mans head, that suffered th'other day,
> Makes him thou'ht dead, through out the citie.[3]

It seems unlikely that Shakespeare, with this way open before him, chose a rougher course—that of making the man destined to suffer in Claudio's stead a living character in the play—that he proceeded some distance along it, only to change his mind belatedly, and hurry back to the road Whetstone had taken, leaving at a very loose end this now unwanted character. This is so extravagant an hypothesis that I think we could hardly do worse if we were to approach the problem from the opposite end. Suppose we consider Barnardine as created for survival. Would not that first audience, who *knew their Shakespeare* in the double sense in which we can never know him, receive the fooling between Pompey and Abhorson as an assurance that the happy ending was to be complete? Even if they were momentarily disconcerted by the Duke's

---

[1] He recurs to Barnardine, even when writing on another play (*The Tempest*). Hazlitt permits himself an occasional critical escapade: Lucio, for tweaking a duke's nose, becomes very nearly a hero to him.

[2] *Shakespeare*, p. 148. See also R. W. Chambers, *The Jacobean Shakespeare and 'Measure for Measure'*, p. 55.   [3] I *Promos and Cassandra*, IV. v.

insistence that Barnardine is to die as soon as he is fit for death, they might recollect that, no sooner was the Duke satisfied of Claudio's readiness for death, than he began to take measures for preserving his life. The Provost's tale, of having tried to bring Barnardine to a fit state by feigned preparations for his execution, would trouble them not at all.

When he beganne to reigne, the people were abandoned to dissolute manners: for which cause he made some rigorous lawes, and other milde and pittifull: but, when he commaunded them to be proclaimed openly, he gave advertisement unto his ministers, to execute them in secrete. Consider not so much what I commaund you, as the intent wherewith I commaund you, which is to weete, that rigorous lawes are not, but to terrifie: but lawes which are pitifull, to be executed, because we make not lawes, to take away mennes lives, but to roote and weede vices out of our common wealthes.[1]

That is a representative passage from a 'life' of Alexander Severus, one of some importance in the development of that legend to which I have referred. It reflects the contemporary idea of the penal code as (in one aspect at least) didactic; and it reminds us that Shakespeare's contemporaries were accustomed to think in extremes: the extreme penalty, for example, or else free pardon. It is surely probable that his original audience awaited confidently the emergence of the real victim, and were not surprised when (true to Whetstone's precedent, and the established customs of tragi-comedy) he proved to be merely a name, without so much as a body to excite sympathy. But they may not have guessed, before the end, Shakespeare's purpose in making nature, not Angelo, pronounce sentence on this bodiless Ragozine.

To all this I see no serious objection, unless it were the gravity of the crime on Barnardine's charge-sheet; and of this we have but the one indication—a single word in that difficult and doubtful couplet of the Provost's: murderer. If this indeed represents the dramatist's final intention, it is surely odd that the Duke should know nothing of it; odder, perhaps, that he, who makes so many inquiries about Barnardine's case, should—as the text stands—

---

[1] Antonio de Guevara, *Décadas de las vidas de los x Césares* (Valladolid, 1539), translated by E. Hellowes as *A Chronicle, conteyning the lives of tenne Emperours of Rome* (1577), p. 441.

not ask for what crime he has been condemned. That Barnardine was never intended to die in the play, I am certain. But whether the qualities that have made him deathless in the imagination of many readers[1] were part of Shakespeare's design, or came from that bounty which he could hardly deny any of his creatures—here lies no certainty, nor the hope of any.

For all its joins and patches, this episode[2] has a dramatic life, and therefore integrity, which are wanting, or but fitfully present, in those that follow. The mechanics of the substitution are readily contrived, the Provost goes out to fetch the property head, and the Duke confides to us an oddly circumstantial piece of information:

> Now wil I write Letters to *Angelo*,
> (The Provost he shal beare them) whose contents
> Shal witnesse to him I am neere at home:
> And that by great Injunctions I am bound
> To enter publikely: him Ile desire
> To meet me at the consecrated Fount,
> A League below the Citie: and from thence,
> By cold gradation, and weale-ballanc'd forme,
> We shal proceed with *Angelo*.[3]

What are we to make of the discrepancies between this and what is to follow? The editors of the New Cambridge Shakespeare conjecture that the person summoned to this meeting is not Angelo but a ghost-character, who has disappeared in revision, leaving no trace—unless, in that mysterious name, Varrius.[4] This commits us to supposing that a very considerable part of the text is hereabouts missing—and not here only; for on this showing the Duke's ghostly confederate was to have played a major part in the unravelling of the play's knot. How came he to leave so emphatic a mark here, and none elsewhere? Will any lesser disturbance serve to explain what is amiss?

If my suggestion as to the proper staging of I. i was right, then the Duke and Angelo have parted, not in the Council-chamber, but at some secluded spot, perhaps outside the city wall. Now, if

---

[1] Readers rather than auditors. The audience too often sees him smothered in farcical stage business.

[2] I.e., from the first mention of Barnardine at IV. ii. 8, to the Duke's contrivance for his reprieve at IV. iii. 91.

[3] IV. iii. 97.   [4] See IV. v, and opening stage direction of V. i.

we accept the straightforward and apparent meaning of the Duke's soliloquy, he proposes that there, where power was delegated, it shall be reassumed. A formal summons, so framed, will carry ominous overtones to a guilty deputy. But it soon becomes clear that no such plan is to be put into effect. The Duke, as friar, tells Isabel that Escalus and Angelo have been summoned to meet the home-coming duke at the gates and there give up their power,[1] and this is confirmed by Angelo, in conference with Escalus.[2] Presently, the opening of Act V will indicate just such a public encounter. I doubt, however, whether we need assume more than change of purpose, and negligence in revision. Suppose, all this while, the culmination to be forming ever more clearly in the dramatist's mind. As it stands, the trial scene shows the Duke deliberately putting Angelo off his guard. I conjecture that Shakespeare sacrificed the good, to the better, dramatic effect: cut out[3] a private meeting between ruler and deputy, in order to secure a more ambiguous, and therefore engrossing, relationship between these two, at their public meeting. It is possible that he contented himself, carelessly, with references to the perplexing tenor of the Duke's letters to Angelo.[4]

Difficulties, however, still multiply. To the Duke come two persons in succession. Isabel visits the prison to assure herself of Claudio's safety, and the Duke lies to her. This, though the most disagreeable piece of his 'craft', is not past explaining: he has cast her for a part in his moral interlude; she is to accuse Angelo of an offence against her person of which she knows him to be innocent. It is only because we know her to be convinced that he is guilty of a graver crime that we endure this subterfuge. This explanation he cannot give, without injury to the effect of the final scene; and that with which he puts us off ('To make her heavenly comforts of dispaire, When it is least expected') is as flat and trivial as the present comfort which he offers her—and which is so unaccountably effectual. Lucio's 'Good even', when he joins them to collect fresh scandal and tighten his hold upon the elusive friar, betrays disorder

---

[1] IV. iii. 132.   [2] IV. iv. 6.
[3] —whether from his manuscript, or from the design in his mind.
[4] IV. ii. 215, and IV. iv. 3. My explanation of IV. iii. 96 to 104 assumes that the change 'I will write' . . . 'We shall proceed with Angelo' suggests sovereignty re-assumed, not, as the New Cambridge editors suppose, a confederate.

in the text, for the Duke had bid Isabel 'Good morning' only thirty-eight lines before.[1]

One further episode sustains an appearance at least of order. Angelo and Escalus disclose, even in their hasty and brief conference, their differing reactions to the Duke's letters: to Escalus[2] it is natural enough that the people of Vienna should have an opportunity of preferring complaints, whether against his own jurisdiction or Angelo's; convenient also, 'to deliver us from devices heereafter'. To Angelo, this provision wears another aspect: in Escalus' presence he can relieve the pressure of apprehension only by exclaiming that this is a madman's project; left alone, he utters his real foreboding.

Now, in IV. v the text seems to disintegrate. The Duke's first five and a half lines to Friar Peter will do well enough;[3] they are clear as to general drift, enigmatic as to particulars, thus informing us as to the character of the part for which Peter is cast, but withholding information as to the words he is to speak and leaving us expectant. And then, suddenly, the argument is lost in a roll-call of meaningless names; worse still, one name more gathers to itself a body and bursts upon the stage. Who is this Varrius? Mr. Ridley's pleasantry, when he suggests[4] that Varrius may be the Provost's proper name, prompts an engaging train of conjecture; but this is dissipated by the subsequent inclusion of Varrius in a scene where the Provost also appears and is called Provost.[5]

Act IV has, so far, covered much of two days, with the intervening night. It was evening when the Duke visited Mariana, night when he reached the prison. It is dawn when he returns to it,[6] and

---

[1] IV. iii. 116 and IV. iii. 154. Lucio's time-reference would be easily dismissed as a verbal blunder, if it were not apparently corroborated by another: at the trial, he speaks of an encounter between Isabel and Friar Lodowick 'but yesternight' (V. i. 134).

[2] I take his 'I ghesse not' for an answer to Angelo's suggestion that the Duke may be mad, although a question has intervened; a few words may have been lost, and these displaced (IV. iv. 8).

[3] True, there is a reference to letters which promises something and comes to nothing; but this probably signifies no more than change of plan and neglect of revision.   [4] *New Temple Shakespeare.*

[5] V. i. Varrius enters with the Duke; but the Provost is given an entry at l. 281, and named in the dialogue.

[6] The hour fixed for Claudio's execution is still impending (IV. iii. 82), though Ragozine has died 'this morning' (IV. iii. 74).

still early when Isabel comes to ask concerning Claudio. It will be evening when Escalus and Angelo part with the words 'Good night' and in expectation of the Duke's entry on the morrow; night, when the Duke confers with Peter.[1] The scene between Isabel, Mariana and Peter, with its terminal line—

> The Duke is entring:
> Therefore hence away—

will belong to the next morning; and the separation of this announcement from the Duke's entry cannot, as I have suggested,[2] be more than formal. In so faulty a passage of the text, a misleading act-division need not surprise us; and we may conclude that, with the departure of the Duke and Varrius, Act IV ends, as it had begun, in a haze of uncertainty.

Now, Act V is generally acknowledged to be almost clear of big textual difficulties. We have come through the worst of these, and so have arrived at a convenient point of vantage from which to survey that problem which the text of the play poses. In approaching that part of it which, like a channel vexed by cross-currents, joins two expanses of navigable water, I suggested that, even here, the defects were not so dispersed as to disturb the whole. Areas which compel distrust may be distinguished, and I have pointed to two: one is likely to begin with the Duke's eleven couplets, which now conclude Act III, and to continue, intermittently, as far as the departure from the moated grange, which ends IV. i; the other, beginning towards the close of IV. iii, includes (again, with fragments of trustworthy text floating in it) all the rest of Act IV— supposing *that* to end on the night before the trial. To these, as the crux of the problem, I will presently return; but there is meanwhile an objection to be met. It may well be said: 'The acceptance of the rest of the play, as recommended in the foregoing analysis, is supported by many and various suppositions.'—To which my answer would be: many indeed, but not so various as they at first sight appear; they have something in common. Those questionable passages, in which I have hesitated to detect interference from without, may generally be attributed to such second thoughts as

---

[1] He had fixed this for 'to night', in talk with Isabel (IV. iii. 145).
[2] See p. 46, above.

might occur while story and presentation were still molten in the dramatist's mind, and be committed to paper in that very sort of manuscript which Sir Walter Greg describes: one consisting of 'foul papers that had been a good deal altered', and were probably to be 'tidied up' in the preparation of the prompt-book.[1] Moreover, in these alterations, a general trend may (I believe) be discerned: notably as the end is neared they seem to be governed by strong and ever more distinct apprehension, in the dramatist's mind, of what that end is to be. To this some lesser and immediate gain is now and then sacrificed—though the sacrifice has not always been carried to its logical conclusion. And, if these minor obscurities and inconsistencies of Act IV are joined with those that vexed the earlier and (in my view) less disturbed part of the play, we shall still find nothing beyond what the dramatist himself might leave in an incompletely revised draft: one in process of condensation and simplification, in which superfluous expedients may be eliminated but not yet wholly effaced. For afterthought begets improvisation, and improvisation becomes in its turn the parent of necessity, since an alteration in a design essayed while that design is in process of execution is likely to throw the parts out of just relation, and so make further, uncalculated and incalculable, alteration necessary. If we bear this likelihood in mind, the suppositions on which I account for these lesser disturbances agree well enough with one another.

It is time to return to the parts of the play which I have distinguished as more gravely at fault. Here, I believe, is something besides that carelessness of which Sir Walter Greg suspects the transcriber:[2] some defect, in the 'foul papers' on which he was working, so evident that he felt himself obliged to turn elsewhere. How should this be? It is, I suppose, possible that, in this draft of the play, the dramatist brought those parts that engaged his imagination to a state very near completion, but left others, which wearied or dissatisfied him, to wait on the visitation of his genius —or, if a command performance impended, on the spur of necessity. Proof that this happened, however, or even firm ground for surmise, seems wanting. But if, when the material for the first folio was being gathered, a sole manuscript of this play survived,

[1] *The Editorial Problem in Shakespeare*, p. 146.   [2] Op. cit., p. 146.

or was available, any physical imperfection in this manuscript would leave its mark on the Folio text. Injury amounting to defacement—fire or water, mice or candlegrease, the possibilities are plentiful—might compel the transcriber to turn to the playhouse, perhaps to some actor whose recollection of a performance in which he had taken part, however indistinct, would give a specious appearance of continuity. It is at least permissible to reflect on what could have happened if this manuscript, damaged in two places, was thereabouts patched with the stuff of memory, obtained from the play-house; if, at some performance still remembered, an interval mid-way had given occasion for the insertion of those eleven couplets;[1] if the introduction of a song had entailed some disturbance of the text in the opening, and at the close, of the scene at the moated grange; and if the preparations for the public exposure of Angelo had been shortened and the actor to whom the scribe had recourse[2] was here at a loss.

By such trickling infiltration from another source, and that shrunken and muddy, we might indeed get a version of the play in which two passages (the bungling at the moated grange and the gibberish about Varrius) would defy interpretation: they do not make stage sense; they will not even allow it to be made of them. Whereas a producer, using his discretion, may solve (for example) the problem of Juliet, merely by disregarding a stage direction about her which he distrusts, he cannot, by any measure of lawful freedom, so present the beginning and end of Act IV as to persuade us that the dramatist's wishes have been carried out.

The close of such a passage, though it may give us occasion for surveying the characters afresh, will leave many questions still unresolved. Only the Duke seems more substantial than before. If we will but take the pains to see him as he must have appeared to a contemporary audience, we shall find little in his conduct that will not bear examination. He is the pattern ruler, alike of learned and popular imagination; not the victim of a melancholic humour, driven to torment himself and others. It is not the text but the

[1] This leaves us with alternative explanations for their awkwardness: Shakespeare wrote them, but, crowded onto an already full page, they were in parts indecipherable; they were written by a journeyman.

[2] He may, as a boy, have taken the part of Mariana's singer.

commentary that is troublesome. His words remain enigmatic. It should be remembered, however, that his actions are almost too plain to us who have the clue to them: they are (as it were) seen from the unguarded side; and, if any air of mystery is to hang about him—as it must, to intimate the aspect he wears for the other people of the play—his words alone must support it. Hence his dark sayings.

The alteration in Angelo agrees with ideas of character to be found in Shakespearian tragedy. Formerly he saw his own act for what it was; now he sees only what it is likely to cost. This seems to have been what Shakespeare expected to happen to a man who should violate his own conscience. But how are we to understand Isabel's course from the Duke's interposition to the eve of the trial, particularly in her relations with Mariana? Her readiness to bring Mariana to Angelo's garden-house has been exhaustively canvassed. The general censure of this subterfuge has lately been answered on two counts: it was a common and approved trick of folk-tale and romance; Mariana was betrothed to Angelo, and Elizabethan betrothal gave the same rights as marriage. Thanks to patient investigation, we do indeed know more than hitherto both about analogues of this incident, and Elizabethan marriage custom. Nevertheless, there is, as Mr. Harding points out,[1] a still unresolved difficulty: *sponsalia de praesenti* (betrothal contract in the present tense) without religious ceremony might be enough for the law, but it was not enough for the Church, and it seems not to have been enough for Shakespeare. Prospero's injunctions will be strict. And, though the law which makes Claudio's act dangerous is a necessity of the story, the view which the considerable characters take of that act is not enjoined upon Shakespeare either by the story or by the way in which his predecessors have told it. Thus we may hold it significant that Angelo is alone, not in regarding it as grave sin, but in his insistence on the utmost penalty which the law allows. How then did Isabel come to condone Mariana's consummation of a merely legal contract with Angelo? Mr. Harding would suggest that Shakespeare took advantage of the general confusion of thought—or at least allowed it to blur the

---

[1] D. P. Harding, 'Elizabethan Betrothals and *Measure for Measure*' (*Journal of English and Germanic Philology*, April 1950).

inconsistency resulting from his efforts to soften the story on which he was working. Now, both Davenant and Gildon aim at weeding out inconsistencies. It is therefore worth noticing that Davenant makes Angelo's proposal to Isabel a mere test of her virtue, leading eventually to marriage—and so does away with Mariana; but Gildon, less drastic in his remedies, has fortified the position of both Juliet and Mariana by secret marriages; time alone being needed to recover stage proofs of the civil and ecclesiastical regularity of these contracts. This Shakespeare could well have done: Angelo's determination to be free of his obligation to Mariana had only to proceed to the concealment of evidence, as it does in Gildon's play. But what Gildon's play shows is, that the wound is not healed by this care: the poison still works in it; Isabel is furthering another woman's relationship with a man whom she has discovered to be licentious and cruel—and that, when she is staggering under the impact of this discovery. I doubt whether her act stands to gain much from legal justification.

That other argument—that Shakespeare was using a device so generally accepted in fiction that it would pass unchallenged—may prove a stronger line of defence, because it refers to the region of the imagination, which, not being subject to reason, changes piecemeal, more erratically and more slowly than regions under the rule of ideas which can be formulated. (That art may carry ideas of good and bad conduct into an age to whose theory and practice they are repugnant or irrelevant, the novel will bear witness.) Thus, *All's Well that Ends Well*, even though it overloads, and strains, Boccaccio's graceful story, yet preserves some faint reflection of the world to which that had belonged: a world of story-telling sessions,[1] in which women might be ranged against men in mimic warfare;[2] over which presided the spirit of sportive ceremony; behind which we discern much older story-patterns, of lovers, separated by the water of forgetfulness and re-united in full felicity as soon as the woman has succeeded in undoing its spell. The mock-warfare implicit in such debates, and explicit in some of

---

[1] There are traces of this convention in the *Hecatommithi*; it is crudely and vigorously exploited in Whetstone's *Heptameron*.
[2] See Janet Spens, *An Essay on Shakespeare's Relation to Tradition* (Oxford, 1916), p. 39.

the stories, remains faintly discernible in Shakespearian comedy: in the ceremonious duel of *Love's Labour's Lost*, the sportive skirmishes in *Much Ado* and *As You Like It*; and it is the hardening and sharpening, the *crystallization*, of this sport into a conspiracy of women, in *All's Well*, that shocks. Nevertheless, it is clear that not only Helena and Diana but all the Florentine women, and the Countess of Rousillon herself, are in a conspiracy together, and that it is furthered by the reputable characters in the play, and designed for our approval.

Although it may well be presumptuous to compare any other age unfavourably with our own, yet we may fairly say that the representation in art of this or that subject has from time to time been simpler, even cruder, than it is now. For example, when a sole group or class of people tells all the stories, or decides what sort of story shall be told, there will be found throughout this phase of fiction a very simple, rule-of-thumb morality prescribed for every other class. In an aristocratic phase of story-telling, the moral obligations of people in humble station will be simplified; in a masculine phase of story-telling, the moral obligations of women, at least towards other women, will be reduced to something like a formula: the whole duty of woman to fellow-woman is fulfilled in helping her to the husband she wants.

It seems clear that, in *Measure for Measure*, we are meant to approve not only of the Duke's strategem, but of Mariana's, and even Isabel's, part in it; clear, also, that former censure of such behaviour—and of the dramatist's part in it—has been intemperate. But it is a costly defence which can obtain no better than the verdict that Shakespeare knew how to turn to account the conventions of an art inferior to his own. Our best hope must be, to discover how the people of this particular play had come to outgrow, but not to relinquish, this particular convention. If they had not outgrown it, we should be little troubled by it.

IV. The Verdict

> Be collected:
> No more amazement: tell your piteous heart
> There's no harm done.   (*The Tempest*)

ISABEL'S intimation, in IV. vi, of the course of action enjoined on her by the Duke has prepared us for that curious pattern of quibble and subterfuge which mars for most readers the theatrical brilliance they acknowledge in Act V. There are certain considerations to be borne in mind while this pattern is unfolding. The first of these relates to this very course designed for the plaintiff: the self-accusation which shocks us, both as a lie and as a slander on her religious habit.

Stage law, it must be remembered, resembles the law of no country known to history. It is composed of elements originating in story-convention and popular psychology; elements which, like the contents of some former sea-bottom, come in time to appear no less solid than the downs themselves. Even un-romantic comedy, supposedly emancipated from convention, obeys this fanciful code —obeys it, moreover, in respect of the law relating to property, surely the most conformable of all to realistic representation. The article in this code with which we have here to reckon runs: if any witness can be brought to accuse himself, the case is as good as won. Such an assumption is implicit in the story of the monstrous ransom from the beginning: when the woman is so far abased that she will not scruple to publish her own shame and accuse herself with the magistrate, the case against him is taken as proven. The same notion is turned to account in Middleton's play: when Phoenix, in his assumed character of agent to the evil-doers, accuses himself of having undertaken to carry out their designs, their defence collapses.

So much for the means which the Duke proposes. His end also must be understood with some reference to popular thinking, but it is deeper rooted in ideas. Superficially, the story of the prince taking action *incognito* would seem to grow merely out of a commonplace wish for royal intervention in particular affairs; but the roots may run down (as indeed they do here) into a profound sense of the need for a union of knowledge and power. Fiction can—and Elizabethan fiction usually does—assume that the lawful ruler commands, within his own domain, power enough to effect what he wills;[1] that, if his will is towards evil, he will seek to gratify his own appetites; if towards good, to do justice—that is, to regulate with even hand relationships among his subjects. To this end, he must engage in an undertaking which develops in some such order as this. He must endeavour to know. (It is in general very handsomely taken for granted that nothing hinders knowledge except state; if he were able to pass as a private gentleman, all would be plain to him.[2]) His own attainment of knowledge, however, is not enough; he must make others know likewise. They must be brought to share his estimate of merit and demerit; it is not enough that justice should be done—what is done must be acknowledged just. Thus his function is (at least in part) didactic: his sentence will be exemplary, demonstrative; and, to an age familiar with more than one kind of didactic drama, a dramatic exposition of his *idea* of justice will not seem too difficult. The Duke therefore brings it about that the trial shall resemble a play. It has been claimed that *Measure for Measure* corresponds in several aspects with the Moralities and Moral Interludes.[3] I recognize such a correspondence only in respect of this *play within the play*, by which the Duke conveys his intention to the people of Vienna. Between his entry and the close, truth, under his direction, threads its way through a maze of error, what *has been* comes to light, and what *should be* becomes operative, despite all hindrances of human ignorance, self-interest and self-will. These two (*has been* and *should be*) comprise the different kinds of knowledge he has sought to attain and now seeks to communicate. The knowledge which consists in possession of facts is enough for simple, popular anecdote, whose

[1] The usurper seeks more power at home; the lawful ruler seeks to extend his power abroad, according to Elizabethan theory.
[2] Alexander Severus is particularly commended for his practice of forgoing state, and making himself accessible, at all times and to all people.
[3] M. C. Bradbrook, 'Authority, Truth and Justice in *Measure for Measure*' (*Review of English Studies*, October 1941), especially pp. 385-92. See also F. P. Wilson, *Elizabethan and Jacobean* (Oxford, 1945), p. 118. Pater had pointed the way.

burden is no more than this: 'So the good king, having seen for himself how the poor man was abused . . .'—but not enough for any representation which is to bear the weight of reflection; *that* requires the knowledge which consists in right judgement of values. To the Duke's audience within the play, both are necessary, and both are new; to us, who have shared the advantage of the Duke's disguise and seen all that *has been*, only the second has still to be communicated. Thus we are, so to speak, a stride ahead; and the dramatist has to solve the problem of holding our attention during the exposition of what we already know.

Isabel's opening of her own case is designed by the Duke to bring truth to light in a particular way: not only to recount facts, but also to show how hardly they will be believed. He has convinced her of the importance, and the danger, of her undertaking:

> Vertue is bold, and goodnes never fearefull.[1]
> It lies much in your holding up.[2]

His warnings wake an echo of Angelo's threat:

> Who will beleeve thee Isabell?
> My unsoild name, th'austeerenesse of my life,
> My vouch against you, and my place i'th State,
> Will so your accusation over-weigh,
> That you shall stifle in your owne report,
> And smell of calumnie.[3]

This is indeed her expectation, allayed only by the hope that, if the advice on which she acts has been well framed, it will do away with Angelo's manifold advantages over her:

> . . . that which I must speake
> Must either punish me, not being beleev'd,
> Or wring redresse from you.[4]

It is well framed; but not in the way she had hoped. It is designed, not to confound Angelo at the outset, but to put him off his guard and so make sure that he will settle into the trap. Hence the intricate web of truth and seeming truth: the words which are to assure him, and with him the audience within the play, that the

[1] III. i. 215.
[2] III. i. 276—that is, the success of the enterprise depends upon the way in which you support your part.   [3] II. iv. 154.   [4] V. i. 30.

transaction between the two of them has been what he believes it to have been—and what he believes she will never be able to prove. To this end she must imply that he has been guilty of the double injury, against her brother and herself; though she evades a statement of the second of these charges. This equivocation is very disagreeable; but, unlike that in the mock quarrel over the rings at the end of *The Merchant of Venice*, it is structurally necessary: without it, neither intrigue nor theme could advance towards the proper conclusion.

Still busily fortifying, by word and act, Angelo's false security, the Duke elicits a reference to the pretended friar, as one who has abetted the plaintiff; and here Lucio plays into his hands, for the information he hastens to lay against this friar lulls Angelo's suspicion. In obedience to the same design, Friar Peter promises that Mariana, whom he now brings forward, shall bear witness on Angelo's behalf. It is not until she is well into her riddling tale that he is disabused, and even then he is sure of his defence, for he believes that *here* he is falsely accused; and so, stirring at last, undertakes to clear himself.

> ... Let me have way, my Lord
> To finde this practise out.[1]

Friar Peter, who has represented himself as ready to vouch for Friar Lodowick, now volunteers that this indispensable witness may be found; and so—former references to vow and sickness alike forgotten—he is dispatched to fetch him, and all is set for the Duke to reappear, in disguise, reputed to be the agent of the discredited women, and acknowledging himself the critic of authority in Vienna. Escalus turns, with his usual urbanity, to Lucio—

> Signior *Lucio*, did not you say you knew that Frier *Lodowick* to be a dishonest person?[2]

and Angelo draws breath.

All this is *very good theatre*. And here the usefulness of Middleton's analogue appears, for it allows of comparison between *Measure for Measure* and a play with an apparently similar conclusion—one which is theatrically effective, and nothing besides. Marston, both in *The Malcontent* and in *The Fawn*, had used the

[1] V. i. 238. [2] V. i. 261.

device of disclosure by means of a masque,[1] but in neither do I find a pitch of expectation comparable with that of the climax in Middleton's *Phoenix*. Marston's spider (Malevole or Faunus) sits complacently at the centre of that symmetrical web he has spun, and has nothing to do but watch the futile motions of the flies entangled in it; nor is there much room for reaction, on the flies' part, to the realization of entanglement. Now, the trick by which Phoenix brings evil intentions to light sustains the tension of the situation until the climax. Having taken service with the conspirators, he appears in disguise before the old duke and the assembled court, and delivers into the duke's hands a document, purporting to be an account of his son's travels, but actually recording the particulars of the courtiers' conspiracy. As the duke reads out, item by item, this record of plot and plotters, Phoenix avouches that he was in every instance the hired agent; the still undisclosed offenders, in ostentatious zeal, spring forward one after another to arrest him, but as each advances *his* name is found in the indictment and proclaimed. There is a flicker of comedy—not unlike that which Lucio introduces into the trial scene—when Falso, who has missed the beginning of the affair and the significance of the document, is flattered at hearing himself mentioned in it. The conclusion of the matter, however, is no more than this: the old duke recognizes his son as better fitted than himself to rule, and abdicates in his favour; and the new duke summarily distributes rewards and punishments among those lesser evil-doers whose injuries and sufferings in their mutual dealings he has taken occasion to investigate.

The Duke's appearance before Angelo and Escalus in the character of Friar Lodowick is charged with more significance than this. It makes intelligible the symbolism of the trial's opening, by opposing its image reversed. On his first appearance, in state, accompanied by his deputies, the Duke had been a symbol of power without knowledge; now he reappears as knowledge without power. Lucio is the touchstone: formerly he was irrepressible, now he is dangerous. The Duke, enthroned but unenlightened, had been unable to secure order; in disguise, he cannot ensure even his own safety. Sitting in state, he had deliberately shown himself

[1] *Malcontent*, V. iii. *Fawn*, V. i. (Bullen's edition, vols. i and ii.)

to his audience within the play as one who, for want of better knowledge, must take the word of a *seemer*, of the man not yet found out—Angelo's word; now he joins the sorry ranks of those who are at the mercy of the informer, the plausible, officious man —Lucio's mercy. He knows now what is behind the fair shows of society: his description of Vienna[1] is rather a token of this shocking discovery than a social document to be taken at the foot of the letter; he knows, but he cannot make his knowledge effectual. He can give expression to the dreadful irony of the situation, inherent in every version of the story: the victim, turning to the source of justice for redress of wrong, is confronted with the wrong-doer. He can, that is, see and speak, but he cannot act—until, with the disclosure of his identity, knowledge and power are at last effectually joined.

The might of false-seeming has been demonstrated and the seemer exposed. Angelo stands at the mercy of his former victim, and the last phase of this Interlude of Justice is now to be played out. It is here that dissatisfaction with the whole play has gathered and stagnated. This dissatisfaction may harbour confusions and inconsistencies; it may be only half articulate; but it ought to be considered and answered: upon that answer hangs another of more importance—an answer to the question: What sort of play was Shakespeare really writing? Angelo's peculiar share in the ending is a precipitant of the uneasy thoughts and feelings which have clouded response to the intention of *Measure for Measure*. 'All difficulties', the Duke says, 'are but easie when they are knowne.'[2] And, while what we have here to unravel cannot be called easy, its difficulty will be surely lessened if we approach it steadily, allowing ourselves time to recognize the component parts and their relationship.

The first and simplest relationship is that between the pardon of Angelo and the pardons of Juriste and Promos. The story of Epitia is one of a group of tales within the *Hecatommithi*, in each of which, when the tables have been turned between an injured person and the one responsible for the injury, an act of signal magnanimity brings peace and good will. The terms of Epitia's own plea are

[1] V. i. 318. Contrast the tone of his former description of these disorders.
[2] IV. ii. 221.

significant: it was, she argues, for the safeguarding of *her* reputation that the Emperor ordained the marriage between herself and Juriste; but what reputation will attach to the name of the woman whose act has caused the death of her husband? The imperial verdict has given clear proof of justice, in sentencing him to death; let it show as clear mercy, in granting his life to her as suppliant. She goes on to praise mercy in a ruler, delicately intimating that, by a reputation for merciful dealing, Maximian will enhance the lustre even of his own name. He is astonished at her goodness, and concedes what she asks in recognition of her merit. This strain of thought is not, I believe, distinctively Christian: we are invited to accept the splendour of a magnanimous act as full and final satisfaction of morality's demand—of every conceivable demand; there is no recognition of a connection between forgiveness and indebtedness, no idea of mercy as acknowledgement of a debt that can never be paid.

Whetstone cannot compass any argument of comparable scope. That he was himself a man capable of compassion, several of his writings show, but they utter it fitfully, almost as though the feeling had sprung directly from his own experience and surprised himself.[1] He represents his Cassandra as, in duty bound, pleading for her compelled husband to the utmost of her capacity, and certainly she convinces the persons in the play that her heart is in the task; but she cannot convince us. We are given no motive for her vehemence, nor the means of inferring any. Wooden figures should not be called on to perform unlikely actions. And no cause is shown why Promos should be pardoned, except that she would be inconsolable if he were not.[2]

Whetstone's plan, involving as it does not only the preservation of Andrugio's life but also an active part allotted to him, entails a more elaborate conclusion than Giraldi's: we are, I think, meant to understand that Andrugio obtains pardon in recognition of his magnanimity towards his enemy Promos. Shakespeare, having brought Claudio to acquiesce in the justice of his sentence—'He

---

[1] This is apparent not only in the tone of his references to the victims of misrule in Julio, but also in passages in his harsher pamphlets—for example, the account of the English Roman Catholic refugees in Rome, in *The English Myrror* (1586), p. 143.

[2] Roilletus' Philanira had been likewise unaccountably inconsolable.

professes to have received no sinister measure from his Judge', the Duke tells Escalus[1]—thereafter sinks the question of his antagonism to Angelo, and restores him at the end of the play simply as one of the four requiring some sort of pardon from the Duke. Now, the terms of these four pardons are subtly differentiated, and two at least have proved liable to misconstruction. On a superficial reading, it would appear that Barnardine is charged with murder, and pardoned for free-thinking. I have already suggested that the gravity of that charge in the Provost's sole reference may be an error; it outgoes in reprobation all other mention of Barnardine. If I am right in this, then we may say that his reprieve is converted, in the general amnesty of the close, into a comprehensive pardon for 'earthly faults' unspecified, coupled with the recommendation that he should, under instruction, seek to understand something of his own nature and situation, as a human being charged with a soul. (The Duke's admonition illustrates the idea that the ruler has come short unless he obtains acknowledgement of the justice of his verdict.) Lucio's offence is slander—that is, evil-speaking whether true or false. He has slandered the Duke, telling an evil tale of him which (Escalus is there to assure us) is altogether false; and for this he is condemned to die. He recognizes death as the appropriate penalty[2]—indeed, he is the first to utter the thought; but, with unquenched effrontery, suggests that a lighter sentence would meet the case. But Lucio has also slandered himself—that is, he has told evil of himself, presumably no more than truth; and his impudent suggestion of a lighter sentence invites the Duke to proclaim that he shall *first* perform an act of restitution by marrying Kate Keepdown. Lucio, still hopeful of driving a bargain, insists that this sentence in itself amounts to capital punishment. The Duke reminds him that it is of this very punishment he stands in danger ('Slandering a Prince deserves it'[3]), but, having shown that Lucio is at his mercy, pardons the offence against himself. Johnson, exasperated by the whole tenor of the

---

[1] III. ii. 257.
[2] See E. M. Pope, 'The Renaissance Background of *Measure for Measure*' (*Shakespeare Survey* 2, 1949). Here it is closely argued that this indeed would be the sentence for *slandering a prince* (p. 71), and that the original audience would expect no less (p. 79). This would cast a sinister shadow on Lucio's attempts to father his own words on the Friar. [3] V. i. 530.

play's conclusion, seems to have been reading this passage cursorily when he exclaimed: 'After the pardon of two murderers Lucio might be treated by the good Duke with less harshness; but perhaps the Poet intended to show, what is too often seen, that men easily forgive wrongs which are not committed against themselves.'[1]

The pardon of Claudio is a matter of course, and that may be why its terms are rhetorical—unless he is pardoned *for the sake of Isabel's dead brother* to intimate that, after the experience he has undergone, he is indeed as one returned from the dead. The reference to the restitution he owes (marriage with Juliet) is likewise matter of course, and even perfunctory. It is difficult to believe that she can be present on this occasion.

Now, the complexity of Angelo's case is thrown into relief by the simplicity of the rest. They have only to obtain mercy of the Duke. Those whom they have wronged are—apart from the Duke himself—hardly more than shadows. Angelo's victims have been at the very heart of our concernment throughout the play. Setting Claudio aside, the intercession of the two women is necessary, to bend the Duke's declared purpose regarding him; and Isabel, whom no wifely duty constrains, must be won to intercede. When Mariana prevails with her, their voices indeed join in a musical harmony; but the mind, dwelling on what they say, recognizes the need to distinguish. The burden of one voice is mercy; of the other, forgiveness; and these are distinct.

To be merciful is to forgo advantage; but forgiveness is not dependent upon advantage, for the victim may forgive the offender even while suffering the offence. Mercy can be where there is not love—unless, love of mercy. But forgiveness is so bound up with love that, where love is wanting, forgiveness cannot be complete; and, where love is complete (between human beings), the one who forgives acknowledges no indebtedness, crying with Cordelia 'No cause, no cause.'

Mariana's plea for Angelo is simple and absolute; it is uttered in one line:

> I crave no other, nor no better man.[2]

It is the plea of love. It satisfies the imagination as Cassandra's could not, for its motive—a love able to forgive, because it has

---

[1] Note on V. viii. (V. i. 504.)   [2] V. i. 431.

survived, injurious treatment—has been from the first, to our knowledge, a given factor in the situation. When Isabel is drawn to join her voice with Mariana's, her theme is mercy, and her plea is so complex, and so intricately related, that its course must be traced slowly, and in its whole context. It does not appear to follow from her former pleading on Claudio's behalf—a claim for forgiveness on the part of those who would be forgiven. Perhaps for this reason, it is open to misconstruction. Johnson turned from it indignantly; and, if his interpretation of the words that offended him is just, the passage is indeed disgusting.

Isabel's argument must first be seen in its immediate context, of the Duke's admonitions and Mariana's entreaties. The crisis of the sentence passed on Angelo, and Isabel's plea for remission of that sentence, falls into two parts: the Duke's injunction (V. i. 405 to 421, 423 to 430, and 438 to 441), and Isabel's pleading (444 to 455), interspersed with Mariana's entreaties. In the brief absence of Angelo and Mariana, which signifies their marriage, the Duke has deliberately renewed in Isabel the sense of the wrong she believes done to her brother; now he takes up his argument: Isabel must forgive Angelo's ill intent towards herself 'for *Mariana's* sake'—that is, in recognition of Mariana's service; but Angelo must die under his own sentence. (Epitia had feared the ill-repute she would earn, as agent of her husband's downfall; the Duke's words emphasize what the course of the story has made plain, that Isabel should have no such censure to fear.) Angelo is to die for that very act which he judged a capital offence when performed by Claudio, and which he has aggravated in the performance by a breach of trust;[1] the law, at its most merciful, is bound to claim that, for a like offence in graver degree, no less sentence than the original can be pronounced.[2] When Mariana, having failed to move him, turns to Isabel for help, he declares that Isabel owes it to her brother to refuse it.

---

[1] The Duke appears to say that Angelo has been guilty of violation of chastity and [violation] of promise-breach. The reason why this latter phrase does not make sense may be either confused syntax resulting from a change in direction of thought while the sentence was forming, or a half-memory of the double breach of faith by Juriste and Promos, each of whom had promised marriage.

[2] This is surely a subtler form of King Corvinus' proposition: I could forgive Promos, if Andrugio were alive.

The gist of Isabel's plea is this: the Angelo who committed the fatal act (of putting Claudio to death) acted in good faith; the Angelo who acted without good faith (in corrupting her) committed, in effect, no act. This is a quibble. We need to understand how Isabel reaches this position. Cast back, she says, to the time when Claudio was alive, the beginning of all this, and admit that Angelo was acting in good faith, until assailed by temptation on an unguarded quarter. (She is feeling her way, impulsively, from suggestion to assumption: 'I partly thinke... Since it is so....') Admit but this, and the arbiter will find that he has erred in supposing the two cases equal: Claudio committed an act which brought him under sentence of law; Angelo merely tried to commit such an act. To treat the evil intent, of which we happen (on this occasion) to be informed, as though it had been born into the world of fact, even though we know that it remained in its own realm of 'intents' which are 'merely thoughts'; to proceed as though it were subject to jurisdiction—this is to trespass beyond the proper bounds of law.[1] Angelo had said: 'The law takes cognizance only of what is susceptible of proof.' Isabel says: 'The law should take cognizance only of the accomplished fact.' As so often, their positions are close together; but they are not looking the same way.

The Duke tacitly admits some degree of validity in this plea by shifting his ground—'Your suit cannot avail, because I have thought of another charge'—as he must do, in order to bring about the final revolution: the discovery which proves *both* of Angelo's actions to have remained in the realm of 'intents which perished by the way'.[2]

Into this plea for Angelo, as into that for Claudio, Isabel has been precipitated by the passion of pity—stirred, now, by Mariana; and this, like that, is a piece of improvisation: she is thinking out her case as she speaks, seeking for a plea that will prevail. Johnson was, in this instance, wrong.[3] There is no coquetry in her

---

[1] To Lupton, this would offer no objection: his ideal magsitrate punishes for intention.

[2] Miss Bradbrook supposes the Duke to be taken aback by Isabel's merciful act. ('Authority, Truth and Justice in *Measure for Measure*', *Review of English Studies*, October 1941, p. 393.) I would say rather that Isabel has brought the argument fairly to its crisis: he can no longer uphold the fiction on which it rests.

[3] Note on V. ii. (V. i. 450-2): 'I am afraid our Varlet Poet intended to inculcate,

reference to herself. Mr. Maxwell observes that Isabel's speech is a piece of special pleading, a gallant attempt to carry a weak case as far as it will go: '... In other words, she is doing just the same for Angelo as she had done for Claudio'.[1] But even this explanation falls short. Isabel is doing *as much* for Angelo as she had done for Claudio; she is not doing *the same*. The reason becomes evident when we compare their offences. Angelo's had been throughout inseparable from cruelty. It has been often acknowledged that Shakespeare's abhorrence of cruelty is absolute. Isabel is his creature. Although she may have thoughts which are not his thoughts, it is impossible that she should claim, in respect of *this* prohibition:

> 'Tis set downe so in heaven, but not in earth.

Her two pleas are therefore like, and unlike, one another. In both, she urges mercy; but this time for such an offence that to use the former terms would seem a mockery of what they had implied. It is the *benefit* of the law she now demands, the benefit of doubt, even of quibble, and the only echo of her first plea to be heard in her second is the appeal for forbearance in the exercise of power. Even that is changed by a reversal of position: she is still a suppliant, but power is now in some sort hers; she has a claim which she can press, or forbear to press. Mercy forgoes advantage. In a lawless age, it forgoes the advantage of strength; in a law-abiding age, it refrains from claiming its legal due. In forbearing to press her advantage over Angelo, Isabel forgoes royal protection, legal security and the support of public opinion; that is the force of the Duke's words to Mariana:

> Against all sence you doe importune her.[2]

By comparison, the Duke's own share in the pardon of Angelo appears strangely simple. It hardly requires to be spoken: the sense of it first visits our ear as an overtone to the discovery and pardon of Claudio, and the explicit reference which follows merely brings confirmation. But then, the Duke himself has taken such pains as

that women think ill of nothing that raises the credit of their own beauty, and are ready, however virtuous, to pardon any act which they think incited by their own charms.'

[1] J. C. Maxwell, '*Measure for Measure*. A footnote to Recent Criticism' (*Downside Review*, 1947). [2] V. i. 438.

are not usually expected of judge or advocate, to ensure that the crime shall remain within the bounds of the pardonable.

It should be remembered that Escalus has already been pardoned for rough words spoken to his sovereign,[1] Isabel, for having exacted service from him.[2] Both these were matters of course; yet both are necessary. In their immediate context, they effect the transformation of that figure standing at the foot of the throne into the throne's rightful occupant, arbiter of life and death. (It is a commonplace of Shakespearian criticism, but still too little regarded, that the work of the play has to be done by words; a great deal of work, sometimes, by a key-word, or phrase: *unknown sovereignty*[3] is a phrase of almost magical importance in this passage of transition from friar to duke.) In the larger context, also, of the whole conclusion, the Duke's response to innocent mis-doing sets the mood for his 'apt remission' of penalties due for culpable acts.

With the completion of this intricate pattern of pardons, the Duke's Interlude is played out. The tension has been sustained, not only for the people of the play, but also for that larger audience to whom the disclosure of what *has been* comes as no surprise. But, as excitement subsides, the question is sure to stir: Are we equally satisfied with the Duke's demonstration of what *should be*? What are we to understand, as to the values implicit in his verdict?

What the simpler part of the original audience would understand may, I believe, be stated as simply as this: Angelo has lain with his own wife, and signed the warrant for the execution of a dead man.[4] This would satisfy a crude and uncritical sense of poetic justice, and even afford some sort of aesthetic satisfaction not confined to those simpler auditors. It would satisfy the general demand for a well-knit story. The true story-teller of every age has power to draw the people of his story into a charmed circle within which, whatever happens is of consequence. Story-tellers, and their hearers, of different ages, differ, not so much in their sense of the necessity for this strong magic as in their reckoning of what makes the centripetal spell binding, and their way of directing—and lending—attention to the coherences by which people

---

[1] V. i. 366.   [2] V. i. 392.   [3] V. i. 392.
[4] This I take to be the reason for Ragozine's fever; no one has died by Angelo's order.

and events are knit. The story-teller of Shakespeare's age, and his audience, found what they required in formal design, which opposed the parts of a story—above all, act and consequence—symmetrically; they were pleased with the patent art by which the event (the outcome of the given situation) was promised, withheld, and at last vouchsafed. It pleased as metrical art pleases, by finely contrived correspondences. It was, of course, nothing new. Giraldi is responding to this demand when he contrives such a correspondence between the act for which Epitia's brother is judged, and the act of which his judge is guilty. Shakespeare is but carrying the same process further when he underlines the correspondence between Claudio's predicament and Angelo's: the betrothal, the impediment of the disputed, or frustrated, marriage settlement. Now, this ingeniously formal pattern of correspondence between the outcome of Angelo's several actions would, I believe, once have gratified a taste now lost or outgrown. We do not ask that consequence in story should be for a while withheld by such dexterous attraction and distraction of attention as makes a juggler's balls seem to remain always in the air, and at length vouchsafed in such a manner that it may almost be said to *rhyme* with cause. That is surely because the novel—and, above all, the art of the great, slow novels that span the nineteenth century—has taught us to look for another sort of satisfaction, and to pride ourselves on a more sensitive response to subtler promptings.

This nicety, however, may prove dear if it costs us the power of enjoying tragi-comedy. The art of tragi-comedy is seldom practised in good earnest today; the time when Giraldi could plead its cause in the high court of criticism is now far off; and an art of which the practice has lapsed falls easily from disesteem to misconstruction. If it is the assumptions of tragi-comedy that should govern our response when the Duke demonstrates the nullity of Angelo's every act, then we are less happily placed for understanding the import of the demonstration than were the members of that first audience, to whom these assumptions were deeply familiar.

Tragi-comedy is notorious for its shifts: for the trick of balancing its accounts by discovering sixpence at the back of the drawer, or blotting a figure near the head of a debit column whose many particulars will surely be forgotten by the time the foot is reached. Its operative faculty is *favourable chance*; to this is confided the turn from unpropitious to propitious circumstance at the very instant when calamity threatens to become irretrievable. And, so long as circumstance alone is in question, acquiescence is easy. Even when tragi-comedy takes similar liberty with character, when occurrences *within* the persons of the story are equally opportune, the imagination is capable of complying. But there is a further region of make-believe, where character and circumstance in conjunction yield to the operation of this less-than-divine providence. The turn by which disaster is averted in *All's Well that Ends Well*, for example, involves a development of character on the part of Bertram, curiously bound up with the event. He discovers the quality of an act to which his will has committed him; discovers it, however, not, as in tragedy, by performing this act, but by learning what it would have cost, if he had not been thwarted in the performance. Seemingly we are to understand that this quality, this goodness or badness of the thing done, can be learnt on easier terms than by doing it. And it is on these easier terms that Angelo must be supposed to have learnt to know himself.

Allegorical representation has its own means of separating the act willed and the act performed: a sort of fragmentation. Closely wrought narrative, unhurried in development, can show the inner motion that is not to issue in action. But Elizabethan drama, with its half-memory of allegorical modes no longer viable, its numerous persons and rapid development of the event, must externalize this distinction, translating one man's impulse into act and moving another man into position to nullify that very act. 'Heaven doth with us, as we, with Torches doe', the Duke has said.[1] In his vice-regal capacity, he has taken upon him to light this particular torch; and he who lights a torch may be able to quench it before it consumes itself.

Moreover, an Elizabethan play which *ends well* demands of us a robust attitude to its people and their vicissitudes; a refusal to let them cheat us of more sympathy than is due to a world of shades; an acceptance of its tacit promise that no disquiet shall reverberate beyond the end of the play. Our imagination is not to dwell on the

[1] I. i. 33.

relationship of brother and sister whose mutual trust has been disturbed; and it is the very idleness of criticism to ask how these new-married couples will settle down together.

So far the conventions of tragi-comedy will bear us; but, grant all that they require, and *Measure for Measure* still opposes to acceptance one immovable difficulty. However ineffectual we allow Angelo's act to have been, there is no denying its performance. Action, and not intention merely, is entailed when he negotiates the purchase of a human being; and that is what his proposal to Isabel means. Bribing and being bribed, like so many human transactions, offers itself to comic or tragic treatment, and there may be an uncharted deep between the two; but the common sentiment of humanity distinguishes clearly enough between the man who bribes another by offering something which will supposedly add to his well-being and the man who buys another in the currency of his need; and much more clearly between both of these and the man who obtains another's consent to an abhorred act by means of his abhorrence of an act equally bad. The coin dangled before a venal official is plain comedy; the bread offered to a hungry and impatient man may be tragi-comedy; there are none but tragic implications in the water held within reach of the man whose child is perishing of thirst. Human sentiment condemns outright the betrayer of his kind who, strong in the weakness of his victim's situation, contrives for him an intolerable dilemma: either issue is abominable, and yet the wretch must proceed as though he *chose*. It is this simulacrum of choice that Angelo has contrived for Isabel.

The stratagem by which Isabel is relieved of responsibility for the outcome may redeem Angelo in the eyes of Shakespeare's Vienna; the deviser of the stratagem may be exonerated by the laws of that imaginary world he was created to inhabit. But to be satisfied with the Duke's position is not the same thing as being satisfied with the dramatist's. The one is a product of art, which is obliged to circumscribe life: moving within its confines, he may propound that, under his care, evil has never developed from potential to actual; and we may assent to the proposition as one proper for him to advance. But the other is of like nature with ourselves; and, if he leaves us with the sense that he has failed to see, or chosen to ignore, what is patent to us, we shall suffer a deep and corroding discontent.

Must we indeed turn away from *Measure for Measure* towards another phase of Shakespearian tragi-comedy: that in which, by a simpler, more explicit employment of make-believe, magic is invoked, not only to disperse evil but also to work upon our ignorance of the very world *we* inhabit, and suggest that the *fabric of this vision* is itself no more substantial than the pageant of art? Between the Duke on the hither shore, and Prospero on his island, run those deep waters upon which

> No voice divine the storm allay'd,
> No light propitious shone;
> When, snatch'd from all effectual aid,
> We perish'd, each alone.

These are the waters of Shakespearian tragedy. Was Shakespeare looking that way when he wrote *Measure for Measure*?

IV

CONCLUSION

'Integrity without knowledge is weak and useless, and knowledge without integrity is dangerous and dreadful.' (Johnson, *Rasselas*)

WHAT sort of play was Shakespeare writing? Three possibilities emerge, like islands dimly descried in the fog of controversy. Until we can distinguish the reefs which, on that iron coast, join one with another, they may be differentiated thus: he was writing of deliberate intent a play that might express, and perhaps relieve, a malign mood; he was writing, of set purpose, a play which should explicitly affirm a benign belief; he did not know what he was writing—or, he began to fashion a play out of materials lying to his hand, and discovered too late of what they were composed.[1]

If we are to find an answer to so strangely vexed a question, we shall have to put into reverse the procedure hitherto followed: to turn, in one motion, from particular to general; from piecemeal scrutiny of the parts to simultaneous survey of all that makes up the whole; from analysis to synthesis.

There are difficulties to be reckoned with, besides the effort needed for a change of direction. In approaching a dramatist of the first magnitude, criticism must take account of the temptation to use methods that have served elsewhere and rest satisfied with its exertions. Eventually they will come short. The dramatist (for example) whose command of his medium is incomplete will devise incidents to convey his intention: the illustrative episodes in early drama betray imperfect realization of the capability of this still unexplored region of art; those of later ages, failure to realize what former exploration signifies, or to profit by example. Such

[1] I hope the preceding analysis justifies my assumption that it *was* 'he' who wrote not 'they'.

episodes remain mere illustrations: they tell us what the dramatist is trying to say; they do not say it. Unfortunately, the meaning thus conveyed is easy to formulate in critical terms. Attention is therefore tempted to dwell on it—and to look for a similarly explicable meaning in greater work. We should distrust our judgement if it leads us to rate high the importance of these illustrative episodes in the mature work of a great artist. When you have analysed inferior or unripe art, you have before you all, or nearly all, that it comprises. Not much of Whetstone's intention, in *Promos and Cassandra*, will escape a judicious analysis. When you have analysed *Measure for Measure*, you have merely made a good beginning—such as to ensure against missing what is there, or reading into it what is not there. You have still to undergo the experience of surrender to the total impression.

Another difficulty comes by inheritance. In the theatre, *Measure for Measure* may be said to have hibernated.[1] And, among readers and critics, the play long failed to obtain its share of attention. This injustice has been, perhaps, too well redressed. The elder critics expected that, in a play designed to end happily, the characters whom this ending was to benefit should recommend themselves—the women by graciousness, the men by gallantry, of bearing. Isabel troubled Johnson's imagination. Coleridge found her 'unamiable', and Claudio 'detestable'.[2] For their successors, this condemnation was not explicit enough. The reaction was proportionably vehement: a new generation came to the play looking for darkness and found light; for negation, and found affirmation. They proclaimed the discovery, in terms strong enough to cause fresh disquiet among those who have not shared their experience. Thus, although we cannot say (as we might of *All's Well that Ends Well*) that a critical tradition is wanting, yet past criticism of *Measure for Measure* has not that stability we ask of tradition.

The play is, besides, one which taxes to its limit our historical imagination. The Duke's estimate of the degree and kind of activity which his high office demands of him—the opinions held by all the considerable characters as to good and bad conduct—

---

[1] See 'The Stage-History of *Measure for Measure*', by Harold Child in the New Cambridge edition of the play, pp. 160–5.

[2] *Lectures on Shakespeare*, ed. Ashe (1884), p. 532.

these must be seen in the light of contemporary theory and practice. The people of Davenant's and Gildon's versions obey conventions as to behaviour which, like stage money, are current only in the theatre. The people of *Measure for Measure* obey, or evade, or defy a code which might be invoked in the world to which its first audience returned when the performance was over. And yet, even from our reconstruction of this outer world of Jacobean England, we must again turn back to Shakespeare's stage. An experienced dramatist will know when he may rely on visual impression to convey some part of his meaning, and where he is to say to his actors, with particular emphasis: 'It lies much in your holding up.' The spectacle which they compose cannot but condition our understanding of the play. The trial scene, for example, clearly holds more meaning than the dialogue alone can carry. To comment on it as a popular device in the Elizabethan theatre is not enough; we need to know what, on this occasion, it signified. And for such knowledge we should require not only a record of that performance in which Shakespeare himself directed the *holding up*, but also help in construing it. The labours of scholarship have shown that Elizabethan acting had its own idiom.

Character, and its power to turn the scale in human affairs—these were long acknowledged to be Shakespeare's abiding concern. Nevertheless, interpretation in terms of character is not very favourably regarded in the world of Shakespearian criticism at present. We have been frightened away from it. Bradley's persuasive charm has made it seem hardly less dangerous than magic. It *is* dangerous. To enter imaginatively into others' experience may be one of the more admirable activities permitted to human beings; to draw the creatures of another's imagination into the orbit of our own experience—this is not admirable at all. And only a very slender line divides the two exertions. This is a pity; but in fact the margin between good and bad, exhilarating and enervating, in the realm of the imagination, must always be fine. Whatever satisfaction may reasonably be sought there, the relaxed mind will never find it. Shakespeare's treatment of character may well need to be examined afresh, with due allowance for the bias which novel-reading has given to our imaginations. We must sharpen our realization of what it meant to fashion character within the framework of traditional stories. Mr. Middleton Murry's admonition is useful:

> The axiom, which has long been current in Shakespeare criticism, that the situation derives from the character is, in the main, a mistaken one. The reverse is nearer to the truth; for the situations are generally prior to the characters. But that does not mean, as some modern critics assert, that the reverse *is* the truth, and that the characters derive from the situations. They do not. They are largely epiphenomenal to the situations.
>
> ... There is an element in a Shakespeare character which derives from the situation; but that element is relatively small compared to the element which floats as it were free of the situation. On this element Shakespeare lavished himself, because here he was, within limits, a free agent.[1]

For all its disadvantages, however; for all the perils of misunderstanding with which it is beset; the study of the characters in their relations with one another—here, conditioned by the given story, there, developing free of it—remains the right approach; and its alternative, a pursuit of phantoms: of inner and innermost meanings derived from word or phrase that has been isolated from its context; of an intention not demonstrably the dramatist's.

From the outset of *Measure for Measure*, we observe the Duke to be charged with a considerable share of the play's burden of meaning. In former versions, the ruler had taken little part until the end. Giraldi, it is true, introduced him at the beginning, but thereafter withheld him during the principal transaction. Shakespeare's Duke proclaims himself, in the first scene, a focus of suspense; in the third, he hints at his design of intervention; by the opening of the third act, he has begun to intervene, and from this point to the end he is almost continuously present. After this, it is curious, and perhaps significant, to find Shakespeare's successors apparently intent on reducing this figure to as inconsiderable a size as their acceptance of his plot will allow. Davenant's Duke is old and weary; it is his Angelo who intends mercy, and marries Isabella. Gildon, omitting the first scene, forfeits the representation of the Duke divesting himself of power, and takes no pains to endow him with authority: when the Provost is to be convinced of his

[1] *Shakespeare* (1936), p. 209.

good faith, nothing less than the contrivance of a special opportunity for eavesdropping will serve. Thus curtailed, the part becomes unintelligible. In neither version does he suffer danger; nor, in Gildon's, calumny. Davenant, indeed, allows Lucio to slander him, but shows him treating the offence with unconcern, and forgiving the offender unconditionally.[1] The absence, from both plays, of 'any thing that's low' makes of his visits to the prison a very genteel affair. We must surely assume that, whatever Shakespeare's intention regarding this character, it was beyond the grasp of his 'improvers'.

And yet, for all those intimations of the Duke's importance whose presence in Shakespeare's play is made more conspicuous by their absence elsewhere, he surely does not declare himself in the way we have come to associate with Shakespeare's handling of his important characters. His utterance is nearer to that of *chorus* than of *dramatis persona*. His 'ancient skill' bears no discernible relationship to personal experience; we do not care how he came by it.

The strangeness of the situation is increased if we bring into comparison *All's Well that Ends Well*. For the King of France, sustaining a smaller part than the Duke's, in a slighter play—one, moreover, which has not altogether lost the remoteness of the original fairy-tale—is nevertheless conceived in an express relationship to place, time and people. His sickness precipitates incidents which form the play's opening—and so forestalls the most troublesome question that the translation of narrative into drama can pose: 'Why begin *here*?' The Duke, on the other hand, seems to have let things take their course for a number of years, and we never learn why he chooses this instant for calling a halt. Indeed, the mysterious urgency of the opening scene may well be designed to establish the fact and divert curiosity from the cause. The King's sickness, moreover, joins the chief persons of the play in a common concernment, of which the degree is very naturally varied, from

---

[1] He comments on Lucio's scandalous confidences in the couplet:
>Virtue's defensive armour must be strong
>To scape the merry, and malicious tongue. (p. 172.)

His pardon is conveyed in the lines:
>Your slanders, Lucio, cannot do me harm.
>Be sorrowful and be forgiven. (p. 210.)

one to another. A brief allusion to it, like a slip of willow, roots itself and stands firm:

> *Second Lord.* You are lov'd, sir;
>   They that least lend it you shall lack you first.
> *King.* I fill a place, I know't.[1]

There is a sense in which we may fairly say that the Duke does not *fill a place*. The context of personal relationships, in *All's Well that Ends Well*, is obtained by that simple but serviceable device, the relation between one generation and another: the King, looking at Bertram, searches his own past for the image of the elder Rousillon; he takes an old man's privilege in his welcome of Helena; he has an old friend who, in virtue of long standing, may take liberties with him. But the Duke is presented in a sort of void: he is of no ascertainable generation; it is Escalus who remembers Claudio's father. The King, however, bears no part in the intrigue by which all is made to 'end well'.[2] And when he reappears, at the conclusion of this business, he is no better informed than anyone else within the play, and is therefore tossed (much like Escalus) from one false assumption to another, signifying his ignorance by erratic intervention.

It is to *The Tempest* that we must look for a character continuously comparable with the Duke, and it is with Prospero that the Duke must be eventually compared. They are alike in that each is throughout informed of all that happens; that he shares so much of this information with us as to bring us nearer the heart of the affair than are those concerned in it; and that, by means of this knowledge, he maintains control of the issue. Where such a pattern recurs in plays of unlike temper, we are prompted to seek a reason for the resemblance.

'It is impossible', Johnson says, 'for any man to rid his mind of his profession.'[3] We might guess, even if the context did not proclaim it, that he is here talking of authors. Whether or no the writer's preoccupation with his profession is exceptionally strong, he would seem to have more than common opportunity of expres-

---

[1] I. ii. 69.
[2] In Boccaccio's tale he does not return to arbitrate, and the forsaken wife must obtain redress unaided, unless by public opinion.
[3] Note on *The Winter's Tale*, IV. iv. (IV. iii. 21.)

CONCLUSION

sing it. It is no new suggestion that the shadow of Shakespeare's experience as dramatist may be perceived falling across Prospero. Taken as a half metaphorical expression of the impress of *The Tempest* on our imagination, this is well enough. Taken further, it requires investigation. The action of the play, Mackail avers, 'is throughout, down to its smallest details, planned and ordered by Prospero. He is the magician—one might almost go further and say the playwright—and the other figures are his puppets.' And again:

Prospero is, as I have suggested, the playwright; controlling, evolving, suspending, varying, interrupting, or resuming the action; the other characters, though alive with the full Shakespearian vitality, being, so far as concerns their action, figures that move at Prospero's manipulation. The dramatist has projected himself bodily into the drama. For once, and for once only, he lets us see him actually at work.[1]

Does this—we must ask—imply something more than the recognition of a sympathy between the dramatist and this particular character—even such a sympathy (able to awake hitherto unrealized powers of delineation) as has been discerned in his treatment of Richard III as actor,[2] of Berowne and Mercutio as lords of language?[3] If so, the proposition will bear re-statement. Imaginative half-belief and stage convention, we may say, together gave rise, in the Elizabethan theatre, to an expectation that the magician who appears as a character in a play shall present some such *vanity of his art* as Faustus and Bacon had shown, and as Prospero offers to Ferdinand and Miranda. By an extension of this assumption (which, belonging to the imagination, is infinitely supple), he is supposed to exercise a peculiar command over his fellow beings within the play; and, even as there is analogy between the magician controlling spirits and the magician conditioning the very thoughts of human beings who come within reach of his magic, so there is analogy between Prospero summoning from *their confines* spirits charged to *enact his fancies*,[4] and the dramatist calling within the charmed circle of his art the people of some traditional story. Without pressing too hard the slippery question—how far Shake-

[1] J. W. Mackail, *The Approach to Shakespeare* (Oxford, 1930), pp. 104 and 106.
[2] E. K. Chambers, *Shakespeare: A Survey*, p. 19.
[3] G. D. Willcock, *Shakespeare as Critic of Language*, pp. 18, 19.   [4] IV. i. 120.

speare consciously associated himself with Prospero—we may fairly look for intimations that he allowed his imagination to dwell on this analogy between magician and dramatist.

Wanting the convention of stage magic, *Measure for Measure* affords no such opportunity for references charged with double meaning. Nevertheless, it surely appears that the Duke's activity in presenting what I have called his Interlude of Justice bears some analogy with the activity of a writer of tragi-comedy, when he propounds a situation from which no happy issue seems possible, and then deploys a power strong enough to avert the expected ill. So, indeed, does the part for which he has cast himself, in this Interlude, with his course throughout the play—active alternating with passive, in each, according to a preconceived plan. I think it probable, therefore, that—whether by a train of thought or some swifter, intuitive process—Shakespeare acknowledged a correspondence between the Duke's undertaking and his own, even as he was to acknowledge, more explicitly, his kinship with Prospero.

How, then, does it come about that almost every reader is coldly drawn to the Duke, and some, even to Prospero? It may, of course, be urged that the introspective and analytical attitude of the writer towards his own art is of recent growth; that, of man's two main creative activities, love and art, literary convention—while it long permitted to the poet the ascription to himself of the lover's part— allowed him no more than a reference to himself as artist, in general or indirect terms; that, when at length the novelist breaks this convention and makes a writer his hero, he remains, for a generation or so, content to show how his writings furthered or retarded the other concerns of his life; and that only within the last century has he tried to tell us what the making of a novel means for him. This is true, but it is not the whole truth. It is not because he is unrevealing that the Duke disappoints expectation, and Prospero hardly satisfies all that he has raised. I believe that there is one characteristic which may be reckoned a constant among those persons who fill any considerable place in a Shakespearian play: this is that characteristic in virtue of which they are deeply *engaged*, and it may be measured by their capacity to grieve or to rejoice, to hope or to fear—in such a sort and degree as shall take our imagination captive. Now, Prospero's degree of *engagement* is much higher than the Duke's. Both are to be imagined as engaged by fear: one, in peril from the spirits he has called up;[1] the other, from the man he has established in his own judgement-seat—it is a cold imagination that refuses its aid to make-believe on the score that the Duke may resume his power when he pleases. Personal fear, however, is the least part of Prospero's capacity to suffer: as a loving father, he must be supposed to experience the pang of knowing his child assailable by mortal ills;[2] but, when we have allowed so much, we have still not accounted for that sentient core of which we are aware, in this character. Miranda's words—

> O, I have suffer'd
> With those that I saw suffer ...
> ... the cry did knock
> Against my very heart—[3]

these signify more than the response of her own 'piteous heart' to others' suffering. Likewise, that

> feeling
> Of their afflictions[4]

which Prospero discovers in Ariel tells us, surely, something about Prospero himself. So remote from common experience is his relation to these two: so much more powerfully does his paternity suggest the creation of art than the procreation of nature, and his mastery of his favourite spirit accord with the poet's command of imaginative forces rather than the magician's of alien beings, that, in the sum total of impression, the compassion shown by his *creatures* abides in our thought as Prospero's own attribute.

No such impression of pity associates itself with the Duke; and it is the more to be missed as the occasion for it is greater—his fellows within the play being subjected to severer suffering than *The Tempest* could properly contain. What, then, are we to conclude about this character? We can, I believe, discern how he came into being, as the good ruler of tradition, his goodness substantiated by accepted theory and popular sentiment. Was he there-

---

[1] This is likely to be missed by modern audience or readers, unfamiliar with all that Faustus stood for.
[2] This surely explains the severity of his warnings to Ferdinand, grievous to modern taste.   [3] I. ii. 5.   [4] V. i. 21.

after shaped by his creator's subconscious preoccupation with certain problems of his art? His function in the knitting and resolving of the intrigue is common knowledge; indeed, it is arguable that this, his most obvious contribution to the play, has been too easily remarked, and its importance over-rated. Mr. Milton Crane's verdict—'He... manipulates his puppets with the success of a maladroit playwright'[1]—sums up an estimate which leaves out of count his contribution to the play's thought. Even a less reflective character than the Duke may be the product of reflection, and charged with the communication of ideas. It is through his activity as 'playwright' that *he* communicates them—most easily to those already familiar with their context. What he fails to communicate[2] is feeling: the impression that he is deeply engaged.

Isabel is the chief of those characters who are themselves engaged, and engage us, by the opportunity and capacity they are given for suffering; of whose sentient core we are keenly aware. And yet our consciousness of it is not constant. From the moment when she presents herself before Angelo to that of the Duke's intervention between her and Claudio, she holds our imagination subject by her alternations of hope and fear. Then she seems to abdicate. Her reaction to the one subsequent event which should reinstate her, the news of Claudio's death, is, as the text stands, hardly more than squirrel's chatter, 'anger insignificantly fierce'. From the moment of her submission to the Duke, until that in which she pleads for Angelo against his express injunction, she *is* insignificant. We may usefully recall, here, the comparison afforded by *The Heart of Mid-Lothian*: whereas Jeanie takes matters into her own hands and, at severe cost to herself, wins her sister's pardon, Isabel appears to relinquish initiative and, under another's direction, to follow a course at once easier and less admirable. Out of her seeming subservience the opinion has arisen that Shakespeare wearied of her; had never (perhaps) intended that she should fill so big a place, or else, had designed her to perform a particular task and had now no further use for her. And yet, in the estimation of many, a full tide of significance flows back into her even in that instant of recovered independence. Here is an extreme, if not a

---

[1] M. Crane, *Shakespeare's Prose* (Chicago U.P., 1951), p. 114.
[2] Failure only if measured by the standard Shakespeare himself has set.

singular, instance of a character fluctuating between two and three dimensions.

I believe that the explanation must be sought through scrutiny of a greater anomaly, within the character. Isabel's chief activity in the play springs from the passions generated by a personal relationship—and yet this *source of all she does* is very strangely treated. The conventions of poetic drama bear hard on minor personal relationships; but *this* is of major importance. It is, besides, almost the only such relationship explicit in the play. Escalus' recollection of Claudio's father hardly alters this strangely *un-familied* world; and, though he is seen entering the prison, we do not see him with the prisoner. As for Claudio and Juliet, the extant text leaves me in doubt whether they are ever seen together. More surprising still, Claudio seems never to speak of Juliet, after that single reference in talk with Lucio. Shakespeare's *improvers*, mindful of those proprieties which are rather social than literary, attempt a remedy: Davenant making Claudio commit Juliet to Isabella's care, and introducing a letter to him from Juliet; Gildon adding a scene between these two.[1] Their officiousness is at least understandable: Claudio's silence must appear an oversight, unless we suppose that Shakespeare was deliberately flattening this part of his composition in order to throw into relief another relationship—and what should this be but the relationship between brother and sister? It is as Claudio's sister that Isabel comes into the play: as the woman who is drawn by a personal attachment into a dire predicament. And yet in her pleading on his behalf this personal relationship is faintly expressed. Many times, in her most moving passages, it would be possible to substitute 'neighbour' for 'brother', and hardly wake a ripple. Not that her pleading is passionless—to suppose so is to fall into Lucio's error. The very incandescence of her fiery compassion transcends the personal occasion, carrying her to a height at which, if she would plead for one man, she must plead for all. By contrast, the sense of personal relationship is sharply, even intolerably, explicit in the scene of her conflict with Claudio

---

[1] Juliet committed to Isabella's care: Davenant, *The Law against Lovers*, p. 161; Gildon, *Measure for Measure, or Beauty the Best Advocate*, p. 24. Juliet's letter, Davenant, op. cit., p. 185; Gildon's scene between Claudio and Juliet, op. cit., pp. 34-6.

—the only scene in which they speak together. It puts an edge on her anger and fear; and it is in terms of their common heritage, and what it entails of participation in shame, that she denounces him. Thus this personal connection, which is the pivot of the play's action, is presented in its full significance only at the instant of its apparent dislocation.

Suppose we should find a single explanation valid for these, and all those other apparent anomalies in this character which have emerged from the foregoing examination of the play:[1] it would surely be a master-key. Let me briefly recapitulate the perplexities that have to be taken into account. When Isabel first hears of Claudio's predicament, her thought follows that course taken by Epitia's and Cassandra's: 'Oh, let him marry her.'[2] But, when she intercedes with Angelo, she does not urge, as they had done, and as all Vienna is ready to do, that the law is at fault if it demands the life of an offender who is able and willing to repair the wrong he has done. Nevertheless, when the Duke proposes to her a course of action whose justification is, that it will commit Angelo to an act for which he may be compelled to make similar reparation, she acquiesces; and this, although she has reiterated to him her abhorrence of Claudio's act. And, if we explain this compliance in terms of her anxiety on her brother's behalf, we are reminded of strange fluctuations in her relationship with that very brother—and even, in the *density* of her own substance.

To understand what has happened, we must take into consideration something that emerges from a comparison between Giraldi's various developments of this theme, of a woman confronted with an abominable choice. Where this woman is sister to the condemned man and herself unmarried, it is assumed that any wrong done and suffered, in her surrender to his adversary, can be repaired by marriage.[3] But the situation that this assumption yields is fundamentally undramatic: there is no real conflict between characters, nor within any character; merely such a show of opposition as suffices for a slight story. The sister has only to say on her brother's behalf: 'Since he can, and will, make good the wrong

---

[1] See above, p. 65, and pp. 119–21.   [2] I. iv. 49.
[3] Whetstone, despite national and religious differences, is in accord with Giraldi here.

CONCLUSION

done, your sentence is too severe.' And to say this costs her nothing. Likewise, when her opponent—bearing down this acknowledged right by might—tempts her to obtain what she asks by consenting to an offence the counterpart of her brother's, the two of them agree that she has but to stipulate for the same reparation, marriage. Thus, the whole cause of her distress is the advantage which strength takes of weakness: the double breach of faith by a man whose will is—for the time being—law. It is a piteous tale. It does not yield the stuff of a play. In those other versions of this theme, however, which make the woman wife to the condemned man, dramatic tension is developed through her abhorrence of the act required of her as injurious to that very relationship by force of which she is brought to consent: she must buy his life at the price of an infamy in which he is to be sharer. This is a dilemma such as we associate with tragedy, because it presents a choice of courses from which there can be no good issue. (Hence, such versions as those of Roilletus, Lupton and Belleforest.) Now, in Giraldi's variations on this theme, still in his favourite mood of tragicomedy, his tales of Dorothea and Gratiosa,[1] romance and comedy are respectively invoked and given power to challenge the assumption that a choice must be made between two bad ways. And, in both, this favourable intervention forestalls any possible distress, and so prevents painful engagement of our sympathies: for, no sooner is the wicked proposal made than something points to the existence of a third door.

Shakespeare accepted the version in which the woman is the condemned man's sister, and unmarried. As an experienced dramatist, however, he could not but recognize the dramatic insufficiency of this situation. It offered him an unhitched rope, one of which the slack would never be taken up; and the only means of making it taut was to give to Isabel a motive for reluctance equivalent to that which forbade the wife's surrender. He gave her the convent.[2] So much may be common knowledge; but, like a troublesome debtor, I must still ask more patience of the reader, before I can show any return on what I have already borrowed. In making this

[1] See above, pp. 33–4.
[2] By the same means, he fastens guilt upon Angelo's inclination, barring the way to love and marriage.

one alteration, Shakespeare found himself committed to a number of others. As to plot, he must prevent the violation of her person; or else a happy ending would be repugnant to moral sentiment. As to character, she is marked at the outset by her sense of separateness: she cannot plead in the terms others use; and no shadow of comparison between Juliet or Mariana and herself ever crosses her mind. What, then, has become of her isolation when, with no apparent consciousness of doing anything questionable, she publishes her fictitious shame, and incurs suspicion of which she cannot count on being cleared?

I suggest that the dramatic centre of the play, until the Duke intervenes, is an abhorrence of unchastity which carries the force of the original situation in which a wife faces a tragic dilemma. The form is changed, Shakespeare having taken (deliberately or no) that one of Giraldi's two channels for carrying the story away from tragedy which necessitates a change of relationship between the woman and the condemned man; but it is the old current which flows between these new banks. The pressure which we feel comes, as in a stream dammed up, from such a reluctance on the woman's part as neither Epitia nor Cassandra had fully known. But this dam does not hold. Once the responsibility for choosing has been lifted from Isabel's shoulders, the obstacle to choice begins to lose its significance. In the situation as it is refashioned by the Duke, it is no longer a factor. Presently it vanishes from recollection. In a world rapidly becoming secular; on a stage which was (by force of tacit agreement as well as censorship) the most secular institution in that world; and in the hands of a dramatist who

> in matters of conscience adhered to two rules,
> To advise with no bigots, and jest with no fools,

it did not offer itself to free and familiar expression. An Elizabethan dramatist of far less than Shakespeare's power could far more easily have conveyed to an Elizabethan audience, within the conventions both understood, the reluctance, say, of Lucrece.

When a story-teller has to devise an equivalent for something in his story, as he originally knew or conceived it, which has proved intractable to his purpose, this new constituent is liable to remain imperfectly substantiated, perhaps because he unconsciously reckons on its retaining the potency which his imagination still associates with that which it replaces. Here it may signify all that he requires, and there, dwindle into insignificance. An echo of this story as it may first have visited Shakespeare's imagination seems to reverberate in that antagonism which develops between brother and sister, when she perceives that he does not participate in her sense of the infamy of consent. But that very sense, and its justification, are so little evident in the part of the play which follows that Isabel's account of herself as one 'in probation of a Sisterhood',[1] seems but a reminder of something lost by the way. It is only when she stands alone again, opposed even to the Duke, that her former separateness seems for an instant to recover its importance.

There is one other character who seems to fluctuate before the imagination: now, to be deeply engaged, and now, when plucked back from the threshold of tragic experience, to lose substance and relapse into two dimensions: Angelo. I have said that we should beware, here, of looking for the traditional comic hypocrite. If Angelo appears other than he is, the process is not simply that of assuming protective colouring—even that subtlest sort of protective colouring that distinguishes the human chameleon. Whereas other creatures accommodate themselves to the colours of their natural surroundings, we take on an ideal colour. The insect turns green on a leaf; the hare, white in snow. But Tartuffe, in a society conscious that its profession outruns its practice, assumes the colour of what his companions profess, and, against the colour of what they practise, becomes 'dévot de place'.[2] The kind of man he would be thought is alien, even repugnant, to the man he is, and it is with something like relief that he proclaims:

> Ah! pour être dévot, je n' en suis pas moins homme[3]

There is nothing here akin to Angelo's experience of self-discovery. What Angelo discovers in himself is a badness which even good things make worse, and which makes good things bad. It is the carrion which the kindly sun himself brings to further rottenness; it is the filth by which the sanctuary is defiled.[4] His expecta-

[1] V. i. 72.
[2] I. v.
[3] III. iii.
[4] II. ii. 165–72.

tion is Tarquin's,[1] deepened by experience: for him the gratification and the remorse are one. Presently, this anguish yields to fear; and fear is a pain which he can at least numb, by taking precautions and persuading himself that he has destroyed in Claudio the only witness he has to reckon with.[2] Are we to take it that he has now no regret but for the cost and that, when the Duke makes him understand that this is cancelled, suffering is over for him? This is to put a construction upon his silences in the last act which the tenor of that part of the play does not seem to justify. The last act, being spectacular, must convey some of its meaning by way of visual impression, and 'lies much in the holding up.' How should Angelo conduct himself?

The Elizabethan audience seems to have delighted in final scenes which offered to the eye a pictorial representation of the satisfactory knitting up of the play's intrigue, an emblem of the happy ending. This final spectacle Shakespeare was willing to give them, again and again, with minor variations. It performed (we must suppose) its proper function with such success that to demand, or offer, an alternative would be counted frivolous. A favourite form for this emblematical happy ending might be called the *device of the muffled stranger*. From the return of Ulysses until the last romance, it has held the imagination fast. Its climax, variously precipitated, is the discovery, in a supposed stranger, of a face at once strange and familiar, the face of one believed irretrievably lost: a discovery affecting those present according to the courses into which his absence has led them. This is the very staple of romantic story or play, in which the unknown is invoked to redress the unfavourable balance of the known; in which, therefore, two and two will always make five. It has the safeguard of long-standing tradition: we are not to ask why the man left out of the reckoning has held his hand until now. Some memory of divinely exercised compulsion hangs about it: the Duke's

I am combined by a sacred Vow[3]

is, like most of his categorical statements, untrue; yet these untruths very often direct our thoughts towards an aspect of truth, and this one may perhaps suggest that the appointment of the

---

[1] *The Rape of Lucrece*, ll. 211–17. [2] IV. iv. 23–37. [3] IV. iii. 149.

CONCLUSION

instant of disclosure is mysterious, not to be investigated.[1] Similarly, the conventions of story-telling allow the disclosure to signify instantaneous and complete illumination for everyone concerned.

Not only does Shakespeare use this device in many plays; in *Measure for Measure* he uses it three times. First, Mariana unveils before Angelo. He had counted on seeing no more of her. The discovery brings disturbingly to his mind the thought of some power at work, 'some more mightier member'.[2] He does not at once recognize all the implications of this idea, but his silence and passivity, when at his own request the Duke leaves him to conduct the trial, indicate the numbing of his faculties by an encounter with one whose reappearance his heart has long feared: from the Duke's compliance with his request until the point (ninety lines later) at which it occurs to him that Friar Lodowick has delivered himself into his hands, he speaks no word, and his intervention here takes the unprecedented form of an appeal to Lucio to furnish promised information.[3] Next, the Duke is unhooded. This, a disclosure of the identity of persons supposed distinct, implies for all those concerned a bringing to light of their past selves: they are shocked into asking—'What have I done, that I should *not* have done, had I known?' For some, the answer amounts to no more than Isabel's dismay at an error which is easily pardoned. Unlike Isabel and Escalus, Angelo has not been, to our knowledge, involved with the Duke; but we, conscious that the Duke is informed of everything that has passed, accept the leap of mind by which Angelo himself assumes that his every act has been observed. So far as it implies discovery of imposture, this episode is akin to the unmasking which concludes and completes satiric comedy—or *Volpone*. But I doubt whether this is indeed what we are to understand by it. Is not Angelo to be conceived as coming, here, to complete self-knowledge, confronted, as it were, by his secret self? The dialogue *alone* cannot show this fully. But the tone of his confession, with its metaphor from divine omniscience; his silence while the women

---

[1] It seems almost to be suggested that the Duke could not have been disclosed without Lucio's uncomprehending but effectual interposition:
    Thou art the first knave, that e'er madst a *Duke*. (V. i. 361.)
[2] V. i. 237.   [3] V. i. 326.

plead for him; and, when their pleading has obtained a respite, his single expression of self-loathing to Escalus—these suggest that he has indeed given himself over: this is not merely the impostor faced with loss of reputation. Last, Claudio is unmuffled before those who had, every one of them, feared that they would never see him again. This, a consummation supremely to be desired, is an emblem of *happy ending* as simple as any trick by which a child is first pleasurably frightened, and then reassured.

Such a device as this is, to subtler modes of story-telling, as rhetoric is to poetry: it can be formulated; it can be taught, and learnt. Why does Shakespeare resort to such simplicity in the conclusion of a play by no means simple? I believe that we may understand his use of this device[1] as an expression of the uncompromising finality with which a great imaginative writer takes leave of a world of make-believe. The mere reader knows something of the pang of extrication; but the writer, whose imagination made that world by dwelling in it, has further to come. Johnson notices something that he takes for impatience, in the endings of many Shakespearian plays:

It may be observed, that in many of his plays the latter part is evidently neglected. When he found himself near the end of his work, and, in view of his reward, he shortened the labour, to snatch the profit. He therefore remits his efforts where he should most vigorously exert them, and his catastrophe is improbably produced or imperfectly represented.[2]

I suggest that this impatience has less to do with eagerness for 'reward' than with a desire to shorten leave-taking. The novelist can express it in his own person:

Come, children, let us shut up the box and the puppets, for our play is played out.[3]

The dramatist has indeed his epilogue; but, in Shakespearian comedy, this is most often used for transposing into another key the relations of actors and audience.[4] Except in *The Tempest*,

[1] Variants of it may be claimed for *Much Ado about Nothing, The Merchant of Venice, As You Like It, All's Well that Ends Well, Twelfth Night, The Winter's Tale* and *Cymbeline*. [2] *Preface*, 1765, p. xx. [3] *Vanity Fair*.
[4] For example, in *A Midsummer Night's Dream, As You Like It, All's Well that End's Well*; and to these may be added Feste's song at the end of *Twelfth Night*.

Shakespeare may be said to unbind his spell and take his leave within the last scene; and, in tragi-comedy, he performs this ceremony with marked formality.

It has been my argument—implicit throughout the foregoing pages, and from time to time explicit with reference to some problem in agitation—that tragi-comedy has suffered in estimation from careless study and incomplete understanding. The remedy must lie in a work of larger scope than this. For the present, I shall attempt no more than the bringing to bear on problems I have already indicated of ideas which arise from a consideration of this one play.

The differing implications of a play that ends happily and a play that ends unhappily seem so simple that one or two items in the account have (I think) been overlooked and will bear re-statement. For example, in a tragedy, both good and bad characters are in a certain sense responsible for the final calamity. That is, we may say of each and every considerable person in the play: 'If he (or she) had not at some juncture acted thus, this could not have happened'. In tragi-comedy, the concluding phase of the action is adjusted to meet our desire that those who are—at least by inclination and intention—good should neither suffer irreparable wrong nor be the cause of it to others. Shakespeare interprets this saving clause with peculiar liberality. He makes it retrospective, and so includes those who profess a desire of amendment—Oliver, Iachimo; and even a character who is moved by no such desire may enjoy the benefit of the event by which his ill designs have been frustrated: Shylock, though he does not share in the final happiness, is (at least to Elizabethan ways of thinking) not ill used. To will, and to do, harm are, according to the logic of Shakespearian tragi-comedy, distinct; moreover, the doer of an ill act from which no harm results may share in the final amnesty.

But though the logic of tragi-comedy may seem slack, in that it does not bind the doer to become 'the deed's creature',[1] yet at some points there is a tightness which frets. The question is not often enough canvassed, why and how story pleases. Indeed, in an age unfavourable to this art, it is sometimes assumed that we have no business to be pleased with it. Story pleases by liberating

---

[1] Middleton, *The Changeling*, III. iv.

energy of thought and feeling. ('Else a great Prince in prison lies.') Its most obvious power is exercised in the region of our hopes and fears.[1] Hence it is distrusted as dangerous. It is not, however, confined to that region. It is capable of gratifying a natural and proper desire to ruminate modes of human experience other than our own. Nevertheless, having endued thought and feeling with the faculty of motion, it tends at last to call them home. Even the most unconventional story or play, contemptuous of formal ending, must somewhere cease. The older conventions—the Elizabethan convention, for example, of *rhyming* the end with the beginning—these merely throw the difficulty into sharp relief. The story of the monstrous ransom, as developed by Giraldi and Whetstone after him, ends by confining the very thoughts it has set in motion. The disproportionate emphasis laid on the final distribution of rewards and punishments seems to imply that here is the conclusive answer to every question the story has raised. There is, I think, only one kind of tragi-comedy that has any right to offer its conclusion as an *answer*: that which alleges truth from outside human experience, truth *revealed*; of which *Everyman* is a signal example. And with this kind we are not here concerned. Our business is with a dramatist who speaks out of such experience as cannot claim authority: common experience, though raised, in him, to the power of genius. The knowledge this will yield is likely to contain contrarieties, conflicting elements such as the mind can neither reconcile nor relinquish: a tension such as tragedy alone can fully express. Shakespearian tragedy, in particular, is fitted to express this tension of contrariety; for it preserves, at its very centre, a core of mystery, something inexplicable; and it ends with the death of the persons whose experience we have shared—an event by which they pass from what we know to what we do not know.

It is nearly twenty years now since Professor Sisson delivered his witty counterblast to the common opinion that tragic elements in Shakespearian drama reflect unhappy experience or pessimism in

---

[1] 'Now the imagination is the most extensive province of pleasure and pain, as it is the region of our hopes and fears, and of all our passions that are connected with them.' Burke, *A Philosophical Inquiry into the Origin of our Ideas of the Sublime and Beautiful: Introduction.*

the dramatist.[1] Even with *Troilus and Cressida*, he maintained, 'it is in the main a question of the artistic problems which Shakespeare set himself, not of the problems which life set Shakespeare'.[2] And, as to his great tragedies, he did not 'degenerate' into the art which produced them; he '*rose* to tragedy in the very height and peak of his powers, nowhere else so splendidly displayed'.[3] I am convinced that the transition from tragi-comedy to tragedy, rightly interpreted, will be found to correspond with an aesthetic, not a personal, crisis; one, moreover, which marks a natural phase in the progress of the dramatist's art towards maturity. For, whereas an art which shirks its own proper development may leave agent and recipient alike ostensibly satisfied—the one asking for more of the same and in greater strength, the other ready to go on manufacturing it; art which ripens may leave both discontented: the artist is unsatisfied, because he has come to ask of the form that has hitherto pleased him an opportunity it cannot afford; and those whom he once pleased are dissatisfied, because they long for the impossible—that he should *do it again for the first time*.

A man who should commit himself to the manufacture of tragi-comedy for the market need never desist; but a man who fills the vessel of tragi-comedy to capacity with thought and feeling will sooner or later find them spill over. It is this overflow of content which seems to me to characterize *Measure for Measure*: wasteful perhaps, but not futile. I do not find in it any intimations that can be interpreted as distrust or denial of life. It requires some resolution to stand up—even under Raleigh's friendly shade—and declare that Shakespeare's Vienna is not irredeemably bad; but I am bound by conviction to maintain that Shakespeare's connection with its people is not the satirist's attachment of disgust, but that quite different concernment which attends the creation of comedy. The persons of comedy have lives of their own, and a relish of them: it is not a question of whether we like Pompey, but of whether Pompey likes himself. The sources of his gratification are another matter, and determined, surely, by the design of the play. The same holds for Lucio; and he is a creature of the occasion in a double sense. He ministers to the occasion, whatever it be:

[1] C. J. Sisson, *The Mythical Sorrows of Shakespeare* (Annual Shakespeare Lecture of the British Academy, 1934). [2] Op. cit., p. 19. [3] Op. cit., pp. 27–8.

CONCLUSION

messenger in Claudio's need, escort in Isabel's; traducer and informer when the Duke's situation requires it. In all this he is like the 'old Vice'. But, with a bounty beyond the capacity of moral interlude, Shakespeare bestows on him what the occasion yields; once at least a vein of irresistible drollery:

By my troth Ile go with thee to the lane's end: if baudy talke offend you, we'el have very little of it: nay Friar, I am a kind of Burre, I shal sticke.[1]

He has, moreover, a function to perform—that of safety-valve. Impatience can escape through him: the impatience, at the trial, of the audience outside the play, which is asked to forgo its advantage of superior knowledge and move at the pace of the audience inside the play. What the Duke claims to have found in Vienna under Angelo's rule is scarcely conveyed to us by characters such as these, nor even by Mrs. Overdone and her train. The passage[2] has been too sharply separated from its context, too often quoted as though it were a summary and sworn account of the world in which the play is set—even, of the whole world as it appeared to Shakespeare.

My argument draws to this point. Shakespeare's unconfined thought commonly transcends the bounds of the story he is using. That margin within which it is free to work[3] is seldom wide enough for its motion. But the shock, the sense of impact, with which it breaks out, varies. It is particularly strong in this play. The story he has here in hand liberates thoughts intolerant of confinement—only to confine them within a close pattern of events. In addition to that which I have pointed out by the way, there is the pattern of ills and remedies which necessarily frames the fable of the good ruler and his design for reform of corrupt manners. And this above the rest appears to promise such a conclusive answer to the question it poses (whether justice be the true mercy, or mercy the true justice) as argument has never reached, and story is unfitted to convey. How Shakespeare came to undertake such a story we cannot even guess: the trains of possibility are too numerous and too intricately related. Let me set out one as illustration.

[1] IV. iii. 187.   [2] V. i. 318.
[3] The margin is most often represented by that part of a Shakespearian character which, in Mr. Murry's phrase, 'floats free of the situation'. See above, p. 142.

He was attracted to Whetstone's play, despite its evident crudity, by its power to suggest a connection between individual lives and the life of the community; between the fortunes and actions of the people of the story, and the conduct of authority, law and custom in the world to which they belong. He was acquainted with current ideas on this subject, and with the most popular of the moulds into which they had been cast. Chance, or the good offices of a friend, took him to the *Hecatommithi*, in French or Italian. He found there the stories of Desdemona and the Moor, of Epitia and Juriste, of Dorothea, of Gratiosa—perhaps of many more, and in who knows what order. So far the succession of events does not very much matter, nor are we vexed by the question whether *post hoc*, even if it could be established, would mean *propter hoc*. But, as we go further, doubts of this kind become alike more important and more insoluble:[1] we are proceeding from such events as may have been known to Shakespeare's friends in the direction of experiences which were never, perhaps, entirely distinct even in his own recollection. Through those stories from the *Hecatommithi* which I have cited as illustrations, and through Whetstone's play and story, ran a current of thought: in each, a man in authority finds his will inclined towards mercy to a wrong-doer by the entreaty of the offender's former victim.[2] When, and how, did *this* question stir in his mind: With whom does the right to pardon such an offence reside? When, and how, did it lead on, and give place, to wider and deeper speculations on the nature and scope of human authority? Was it something latent in Giraldi's ideal of magnanimity, or in Whetstone's concern with civic responsibility, that yielded the great debate of mercy and justice—or was it the product of their union? Did abhorrence of Lupton's merciless morality determine its development? Where and when, in this train of events, was the project formed, of employing that oldest,

[1] 'In *Measure for Measure* as in *Troilus and Cressida*, Shakespeare tried to make a philosophical (or theological) play by loading philosophical analysis upon a simple source plot which he patched up in the easygoing fashion of the romantic comedies. The result was simply confusion.' V. K. Whitaker, 'Philosophy and Romance in Shakespeare's "Problem" Comedies' (*The Seventeenth Century: Studies* by R. F. Jones and Others, Stanford U.P., 1951, p. 354). I cannot find this 'simplicity' either in Shakespeare's 'sources', or in what he made of them.

[2] Mariana may in one respect be regarded as Andrugio's counterpart: by her forgiveness of a personal injury she wakes the impulse to mercy in another.

yet most youthful, of story-patterns, the visit of the disguised prince—and so harnessing the power of hope to move the imagination? Was it the consummation of this story, in the union of knowledge and power, which brought Shakespeare face to face with the question: *What sort of knowledge?*

One sort, the self-knowledge which is the basis of integrity, is gained through tragic experience by Angelo and Isabel, and surely by Claudio also. What happens to him illustrates the subtle difference between true and false tragi-comedy. His courage, the very attribute on which such a man would pride himself, breaks—like Angelo's self-control—and he goes into darkness. He had no predecessors there: the pleading of Vico and Andrugio is merely the means to an end regarded as permissible. It is, moreover, significant that he had no successors either: Shakespeare's 'improvers' took care to obliterate this painful impression. Strong in the conventional assurance that no *sympathetic* character is ever afraid to die, they made Claudio protest that any reluctance he might feel was on Juliet's account.[1] In *Measure for Measure* alone we are brought to recognize that this fear is incalculable, and, coming attended by hope, may prove uncontrollable; that it varies in no direct proportion with other components of character—not even with courage. It is not by the difference between courage and the want of it that Claudio and Barnardine are divided.

Claudio's development is to be inferred from what the Provost and the Duke say of him, and that is not much. Indeed, like more important matters, it is left largely to the actor's art and the audience's imagination. This incomplete synthesis has troubled critics. Mr. Clifford Leech finds the play a tangle of unresolved contrarieties.[2] That *Measure for Measure* will continue to perplex us is likely enough; but of one thing I am sure: through its course thought and feeling run like a spring tide into an estuary, with such vehemence that the filth and rubbish, the cabbage stalks and dead cats which are all that adverse criticism has remarked in it, are washed up and left behind as the ebb scours the channel and

[1] Both are guilty of falsification: they use the terrible and moving words of Claudio's appeal, and the beginning of Isabel's protest—only to explain them away as a misunderstanding. See Davenant, *The Law against Lovers*, pp. 160-2; Gildon, *Measure for Measure, or Beauty the Best Advocate*, pp. 23-4.

[2] 'The "Meaning" of *Measure for Measure*' (*Shakespeare Survey*, 3, 1950).

CONCLUSION 163

the volume of water makes towards its own place. This tidal refuse is a sign, not of languid attention on the dramatist's part, but of a force so turbulent that considerable items are overlooked and forgotten as he presses on to his consummation. There is, for example, Isabel's behaviour in furthering—to put the best construction on her act—Mariana's unpropitious marriage: behaviour governed by a code which the character has already outgrown before it is called for. There is the Duke's behaviour in promoting the affair; and this, though it obeys the convention within which he was framed, suits ill with the prevailing impression of his association, in some phases of his development, with the dramatist himself. These anomalies remain, as though left by impatience or negligence, in the pools and shallows of the fourth act. They are neglected (I believe) because the theme of the play, working in Shakespeare's imagination, gained power to 'awaken those ideas which slumber in the heart'.[1] And those ideas, liberated in and by the very act of creation, were hurrying him on—immediately to the fifth act, with its larger scope for expressing them; ultimately, beyond the play's proper bounds.

Let me illustrate this unlooked-for liberation. The initial situation contains one particular—Isabel's religious profession—which seems to originate in dramatic expediency; to have been devised merely to provide sufficient motive for her reluctance. But this circumstance, affording opportunity for the expression of thoughts rarely uttered on Shakespeare's stage, liberates those that lie deepest of all.

> Why all the soules that were, were forfeit once,
> And he that might the vantage best have tooke,
> Found out the remedie.

The play leaves many questions unanswered at the close. Yet its form suggests that it should undertake to answer its own questions, after its own fashion; for tragi-comedy may be likened to a fountain, whose waters, controlled by secret mechanism, follow a graceful course and return sparkling to the smooth basin from which they appear to rise. Its problems contain their proper solution, and both are conceived in terms agreeable to its peculiar

[1] Johnson, *Lives of the Poets* (ed. Birkbeck Hill, I, 459).

M*

mode of expression. But the mind, under pressure of experience, conceives quite other questions. Of these, some appear unanswerable because we have not the means of measuring what they are about: conflicting claims or obligations, for example. Others forbid an answer; such as the question asked of the unforgiving servant.[1] The experience of artistic creation exerts its own pressure, moves its own questions. Not only will some of these be likewise unanswerable; they may, even as questions, fail of complete expression within the scope of that very work which has compelled their utterance.

It is surely not to be wondered at that a play in which questions obtain partial utterance and uncertain answer should fluctuate as to the volume of its power; nor that a play which so fluctuates should be misconstrued. Indeed, any hasty interpretation of *Measure for Measure*, or any which hardens into formula, is likely to approach misconstruction. By nothing short of resolutely sustained attention can both these besetting errors be warded off: that which will make of every anomaly to be found in it a sort of treachery on the dramatist's part, and that which will remove every such anomaly out of sight. Neither representation gives a true portrait of this great, uneven play; for neither allows us to recognize that in its very complexity is to be found the proof of its integrity.

[1] St. Matthew xviii. 33.

APPENDIX

P. 55. *Names of Characters*

The Duke is called *Vincentio* in the list of *dramatis personae*, and nowhere else; nor does the name occur among the known sources and analogues of the play. Johnson inferred that it must have strayed into this list from a lost version of the story. The editors of the New Cambridge Shakespeare attribute this, with other discrepancies, to 'a form of the play different from that which has come down to us.'

The Folio attaches lists of Actors' (i.e., characters') names to seven plays. Mr. Crompton Rhodes supposes them to derive from papers which served some useful purpose in the theatre, as 'a remembrancer for casting, or as a catalogue to a bundle of written parts.' (*Shakespeare's First Folio*, Oxford, 1923, p. 118.) This supposition as to their provenance does not necessarily connect them with the dramatist, and the list for *Measure for Measure* contains one word to which there is no Shakespearian parallel. Lucio is called 'a fantastique'—meaning, presumably, a fop. Shakespeare uses the adjective fantastic in a corresponding sense: 'To be fantastic may become a youth' (*Two Gentlemen*, II. vii. 47); but his form for the noun is fantastico: 'such antic, lisping, affecting fantasticoes' (*Romeo and Juliet*, II. iv. 30). I believe that we should not associate this list with him, nor build on it any surmise as to the form in which he found his plot, or left his play.

P. 79. *Informing the Audience*

> Then Isabell live chaste, and brother die;
> "More then our Brother, is our Chastitie. (II. iv. 184, 5)

These lines seem to mark a curious change of tone, and an observation by R. W. Chambers on a similarly impersonal couplet may be relevant: lecturing on *King Lear*, he suggested that Cordelia's lines

> For thee, oppressed king, am I cast down;
> Myself could else out-frown false fortune's frown—

were designed as a direct intimation to the audience that Shakespeare intended to depart from the well-known traditional story, which had ended with Cordelia's despair and suicide. ('*King Lear*', W. P. Ker Memorial Lecture, Glasgow, 1939 (1940), p. 23.) Such an interpretation should hold good likewise for Isabel's lines, placed at that very turn in the story which, in former versions, had preceded the woman's surrender to the condemned man's entreaties. The couplet is surely delivered to the audience; it may be designed principally to enlighten them as to the new course the story is to take.

Likewise, the rhetorical emphasis of Isabel's assertion to the disguised Duke—'I had rather my brother die by the Law, then my sonne should be unlawfullie borne' (III. i. 193)—may serve as an intimation that there is not to be, even after passion has abated, any capitulation.

P. 83. *Claudio's Fears*

> ... to be worse then worst
> Of those, that lawlesse and incertaine thought,
> Imagine howling ... (III. i. 126)

The difficulty raised by commentators—that Claudio's fear of hell accords ill with the scepticism which they find in *uncertain* and *imagine*—is cleared away if we assume that he refers to a forbidden superstition.

It is well known that the denial of purgatory in reformed doctrine entailed new teaching as to the nature of apparitions: they might no longer be regarded as souls returned from the dead. Such a warning seems implicit in Harrison's version of Hector Boethius when he reports the sounds of wailing heard about the *dolorous mount* of Stirling: '... right lamentable noise & cries, as though the same had beene of some creatures that had bewailed their miserable cases: which undoubtedlie was the crafty illusions of wicked spirits, to keepe mens minds still oppressed in blind errors and superstitious fancies.' (This is fuller and more emphatic than the original, or Bellenden's translation.) Petrus Thyraeus the Jesuit, on the other hand, mentions these very haunters of Stirling among spirits that may be either souls from hell or purgatory, or else demons. (See Hector Boethius' *Scotorum Historiae*, Bk. iv; the Description of Scotland in Holinshed's Chronicle (1586); Petrus Thyraeus, *Loca Infesta* (Cologne, 1598), I. i. See also Dr. Dover Wilson's studies on the ghost in *Hamlet*, and his sources: Lavater, Scot, etc.

Claudio is (I believe) speaking of sounds, supposedly supernatural, in which he fears, but is forbidden, to hear the voices of the unhappy dead.

P. 106. *Passage between the Duke and Isabel*

These lines (IV. i. 26–50) would be satisfactory, if it were not for the disorder of ll. 34–6.

> There have I made my promise, upon the
> Heavy midle of the night, to call upon him.

The Folio's line-division betrays disturbance.

This part of the passage, however, might rank with the rest, if it were admitted that at least one whole line and one incomplete line are missing between l. 33 and l. 34. The sense demands this supposition: Isabel's tale proceeds from the outer wall and the vineyard to the inner wall and the garden, and there halts. But, a garden in the middle of the night being an unlikely destination, we may surely take it that something is wanting and the lines should run more like this:

> Which from the Vineyard to the Garden leades,
> ... (one or more lines missing) ...
> [His garden-house] there have I made my promise
> Upon the heavy midle of the night,
> To call upon him.

Mariana's reference, at V. i. 212, supports this surmise.

P. 108. *Time-references to Claudio's Execution* (IV. ii)

The Provost commands Abhorson to have ready axe and block by 'to morrow, foure a clocke' (IV. ii. 56), and bids Claudio prepare himself for death at eight (IV. ii. 67). The sequel to this is Angelo's urgent missive: Claudio is to be executed by four, and his head delivered by five (IV. ii. 124).

I take it that 'eight' should stand in the first, to correspond with the second, reference, and that Angelo is putting forward the time of the execution, that he may be beforehand with Isabel. A small and natural piece of officiousness on a transcriber's part would lead to the 'correction' (eight to four) in that one passage where a discrepancy with Angelo's order had happened to catch his eye.

INDEX

i. GENERAL

Albrecht, L., *Neue Untersuchungen zu Shakespeares 'Mass für Mass'*, 7, 32, 109
Alexander Severus, legend of, 101, 112, 123
Augustine, St., *De Sermone Domini in Monte*, 6
Bagehot, Walter, *Literary Studies*, 72
Baldwin, T. W., *William Shakspere's Small Latine and Lesse Greeke*, 80
Ball, R. H., *'Epitia' and 'Measure for Measure'*, 7, 32
Battenhouse, R. W., *'Measure for Measure* and Christian Doctrine of the Atonement', 41, 100
Beard, C. A., *The Office of Justice of the Peace in England*, 62
Beard, Thomas, *The Theatre of God's Judgements*, 25, 34
Belleforest, François de, *Histoires Tragiques*, 24–5, 29, 37, 46, 55, 75, 88, 151
Besaucèle, L. B. de, J-B. *Giraldi, Etude sur l'Evolution des Théories Littéraires en Italie au XVIe Siècle*, 9
Bethell, S. L., *Shakespeare and the Popular Dramatic Tradition*, 100
Boccaccio, Giovanni, *Decameron*, 9, 16, 120, 144
Bradbrook, M. C., 'Authority, Truth and Justice in *Measure for Measure*', 41, 123, 132
— 'Shakespeare and the Use of Disguise in Elizabethan Drama', 41
Browning, Robert, *Instans Tyrannus*, 97
Bryskett, Lodowick, *A Discourse of Civill Life*, 49, 61
Budd, F. E., 'Rouillet's *Philanira* and Whetstone's *Promos and Cassandra*', 7, 8, 16, 32
— 'Material for a Study of the Sources of Shakespeare's *Measure for Measure*', 7, 32
Burke, Edmund, *A Philosophical Inquiry into the Origin of our Ideas of the Sublime and Beautiful*, 158
Campbell, O. J., *Shakespeare's Satire*, 26
Chambers, E. K., *Shakespeare, A Survey*, 100–1, 145
— *William Shakespeare*, 44, 58
Chambers, R. W., *The Jacobean Shakespeare and 'Measure for Measure'*, 41, 82, 111, 165
Chappuys, Gabriel, *Cent Excellentes Nouvelles* (translation of *Hecatommithi*), 12
Child, F. J., *English and Scottish Ballads*, 4
Child, Harold, see New Cambridge edition of *Measure for Measure*
Clark, G. N., 'Edward Grimeston', 25
Coghill, N., 'The Basis of Shakespearian Comedy', 17

INDEX

Coleridge, Samuel Taylor, 140
Collier, J. P., *Shakespeare's Library*, 15
Crane, Ralph, 44
Danett, Thomas, *The Historie of Philip de Commines*, 25
Davenant, William, *The Law against Lovers*, 27-8, 60, 72, 120, 141, 142-3, 149, 162
Division into acts and scenes, in *M. for M.*, 44-6
Dodds, W. M. T., 'The Character of Angelo in *Measure for Measure*', 41, 74
Donne, John, *Bianthanatos*, 6
Douce, Francis, *Illustrations of Shakespeare*, 6, 7, 21
Dramatis personae, list of, in *M. for M.*, 55-6, 165
Eliot, George, *Middlemarch*, 73
Elyot, Thomas, *The Boke named the Governour*, 69
— *The Image of Governance*, 101
Empson, W., *The Structure of Complex Words*, 42
Estienne, Henri, *Apologie pour Hérodote*, 25
Everyman, 158
Farmer, J. S., *Tudor Facsimile Texts*, 13
Farnham, W., *Medieval Heritage of Elizabethan Tragedy*, 80
— *Shakespeare's Tragic Frontier*, 6
Fielding, Henry, and *Pamela*, 37
Fletcher, John, *The Bloody Brother*, 105
Freeburg, V. O., *Disguise Plots in Elizabethan Drama*, 27
Gildon, Charles, *Measure for Measure, or Beauty the Best Advocate*, 27-8, 72, 120, 141, 142-3, 149, 162
Giraldi, Celso, 13
Giraldi Cinthio, Giovanbattista, life, 9
— *Dialoghi della vita Civile*, 10, 49
— *Discorsi*, 10
— *Epitia*, 12-13, 17-18
— *Hecatommithi*, 9-12, 19, 29, 32-6, 42, 46, 55, 59, 65, 75, 120, 127-8, 150-1, 161
Goulart, Simon, *Histoires Admirables et Memorables*, 25, 88
Greg, W. W., *The Editorial Problem in Shakespeare*, 44, 117
Grimeston, Edward, *Admirable and Memorable Histories*, 25
Guevara, Antonio de, 101, 112
Halliwell-Phillipps, J. O., *Memoranda on Shakespeare's Comedy of Measure for Measure*, 21
Harding, D. P., 'Elizabethan Betrothals and *Measure for Measure*', 38, 119
Hazlitt, William, 26, 72, 111
Hazlitt, W. C., *Shakespeare's Library*, 13, 15
Holinshed, Raphael, *Chronicles*, 166
Izard, T. C., *George Whetstone*, 14, 15
James I, 108-9
Johnson, Samuel, opinions on *Measure for Measure*, 43, 63, 80, 106, 129-33
— on other subjects, 1, 21, 83, 144, 156
Jones, L. C., *Simon Goulart*, 25
Jump, J. D., edition of Fletcher's *Bloody Brother*, 105

INDEX

Justice of the Peace, office of, 62
Keeton, G. W., *Shakespeare and his Legal Problems*, 49, 63
Knight, G. Wilson, *The Wheel of Fire*, 41, 99
Lawrence, W. W., *Shakespeare's Problem Comedies*, 26, 38
Leavis, F. R., 'The Greatness of *Measure for Measure*', 41, 100
Leech, C., 'The "Meaning" of *Measure for Measure*', 162
Lennox, Charlotte, *Shakespear Illustrated*, 12, 82, 84
Lupton, Thomas, *Siuqila, Too good, to be true*, 21
— *The Second part . . . of the Boke entituled Too good to be true*, 21-4, 29, 36-7, 96, 98, 102, 132, 151, 161
Mackail, J. W., *The Approach to Shakespeare*, 145
Marston, John, *The Fawn*, 26, 125
— *The Malcontent*, 26, 125
Martin, L. C., 'Shakespeare, Lucretius and the Commonplaces', 80, 83
Maxwell, J. C., '*Measure for Measure*, A Footnote to Recent Criticism', 41, 133
Middleton, Thomas, *The Changeling*, 157
— *Phoenix*, 26-7, 102-3, 122, 125-6
Molière, *Tartuffe*, 153
Moral Interlude, in *M. for M.*, 95, 123
More, Thomas, *Utopia*, 22
Murry, J. Middleton, *Shakespeare*, 142, 160
New Cambridge Shakespeare, edition of *Measure for Measure*, 43, 45, 47, 50-1, 53, 54, 63, 71, 76, 140
Nichols, J., *Six Old Plays*, 13
Paris, Gaston, 'Le Cycle de la Gageur', 4
Pater, Walter, '*Measure for Measure*', 41, 88, 89, 123
Pope, E. M., 'The Renaissance Background of *Measure for Measure*', 129
Quiller-Couch, Arthur, see New Cambridge edition of *Measure for Measure*
Raleigh, Walter, *Shakespeare*, 39, 78, 111
Rhodes, R. Crompton, *Shakespeare's First Folio*, 165
Ridley, M. R., edition of *Measure for Measure*, New Temple Shakespeare, 115
Roilletus, Claudius, *Philanira*, 8-9, 16, 21, 29, 128, 151
— *Varia Poemata*, 8
Royal Proclamations, 49-50
Scott, Walter, *The Heart of Mid-Lothian*, 84-8, 148
Sidney, Philip, *Arcadia*, 38
Sisson, C. J., *The Mythical Sorrows of Shakespeare*, 158-9
Smith, R. M., 'Interpretations of *Measure for Measure*', 41
Spens, J., *An Essay on Shakespeare's Relation to Tradition*, 120
Thackeray, William Makepeace, *Vanity Fair*, 156
Tillyard, E. M. W., *Shakespeare's Problem Plays*, 84
Traversi, D. A., '*Measure for Measure*', 41, 100
Warburton, William, edition of Shakespeare, 68, 107
Whetstone, George, life, 14, 15
— *Aurelia*, 15
— *The Censure of a Loyall Subject*, 14

Whetstone, George (*cont.*), *The English Myrror*, 14, 62, 128
— *An Heptameron*, 15–16, 19, 120, 161
— *The Honorable Reputation of a Souldier*, 14
— *A Mirour for Magestrates of Cyties*, 96, 101
— *Promos and Cassandra*, 13–21, 29, 32, 51, 59–60, 96, 99, 111, 128, 140, 161
— *The Rocke of Regard*, 14
— *A Touchstone for the Time*, 14
Whitaker, V. K., 'Philosophy and Romance in Shakespeare's "Problem" Comedies', 100, 161
Willcock, G. D., *Shakespeare as Critic of Language*, 31, 145
Wilson, F. P., *Elizabethan and Jacobean*, 123
— 'Ralph Crane, Scrivener to the King's Players', 44
— 'Shakespeare's Reading', 30, 36
Wilson, J. Dover, *The Fortunes of Falstaff*, 42
— edition of Henry VI, 49
— edition of *Measure for Measure*, see New Cambridge Shakespeare
Wolff, S. L., *Greek Romances in Elizabethan Prose Fiction*, 18

ii. References to Poems and Plays of Shakespeare other than 'Measure for Measure'

All's Well that Ends Well, 56, 77, 120–121, 136, 140, 143–4, 156
Antony and Cleopatra, 107
As You Like It, 78, 121, 156, 157
Cymbeline, 4, 38, 78, 107, 156, 157
Hamlet, 65, 81
Henry VI, 49
Henry VIII, 50
Julius Caesar, 78, 106
King John, 78
King Lear, 82, 165
Love's Labour's Lost, 121, 145
Macbeth, 73, 78
Merchant of Venice, The, 66, 125, 156, 157
Midsummer Night's Dream, A, 86, 156
Much Ado about Nothing, 121, 156
Othello, 24, 36, 37, 73, 161
Pericles, 103
Rape of Lucrece, The, 154
Richard III, 145
Romeo and Juliet, 49, 78, 79, 145, 165
Tempest, The, 104, 138, 144–7
Troilus and Cressida, 159
Twelfth Night, 78, 156
Two Gentlemen of Verona, The, 165
Winter's Tale, The, 78, 156